TIGER, BURNING BRIGHT

More Myths than Truths about Korean Tigers

TIGER, BURNING BRIGHT

Kathleen J. Crane Foundation

HOLLYM

Copyright © 1992
by Kathleen J. Crane Foundation

All rights reserved

First published in 1992
by Hollym International Corp.
18 Donald Place, Elizabeth, New Jersey 07208 USA
Phone: (908)353-1655   Fax: (908)353-0255

Published simultaneously in Korea
by Hollym Corporation; Publishers
14-5 Kwanchol-dong, Chongno-gu, Seoul 110-111, Korea
Phone: (02)735-7554   Fax: (02)730-5149

Hard cover edition ISBN: 1-56591-003-6
Paperback edition ISBN: 1-56591-004-4
Library of Congress Catalog Card Number : 92-75873

Illustrated by Byoung-ho Han

Printed in Korea

*In honor of Professor Yeon-ok Kim
now retired after being teacher, friend
and mentor to scores of thousand
students throughout her four decades of
dedicated service at Ewha Womans
University in Seoul.*

PREFACE

Tigers have always had a special place in the hearts of Koreans. Having had to share their habitat with the most terrible animal from time immemorial, Koreans have spun myths and tales around the animal that made it their friend, guardian and mentor. Perhaps it was a clever survival strategy to turn their deadly enemy into their benefactor and guardian angel, even if they knew it was only wishful thinking. But more probably it was that Koreans refused to regard a being of such noble form and marvelous strength as a mere rapacious beast, and wanted it to possess nobility and magnanimity surpassing not only a mere animal but even human beings—almost a god, in fact. On the other hand, Koreans also wanted the lofty animal to have a few weaknesses, too, so they could reason with, cajole, even hoodwink it: a being they could patronize or take advantage of, with luck, pluck, and wit. In short, Koreans have tamed the tiger and made it almost a household pet in their imagination. No other country has the concept of the funny or the laughing tiger.

Professor Yi Ka-won has collected a number of the innumerable tiger stories handed down in many parts of the country. The translations in this book are based on Professor Yi's collection. They are grouped according to their themes or subjects: the tiger's character and habits, the tiger as man's best friend, the tiger as man's moral guide, the tiger as a humble, grateful animal, the tiger as a greedy and stupid animal justly punished by men. Of course the tales are not so much portrayals of tigers as of Koreans—what Koreans want from life and what they want from fellow inhabitants, human and animal, of their land. The tales are fantastic, amusing, even chastening. And they testify to the optimism and lust for life of old Koreans.

These tales have been translated by graduates of the English Department of Ewha Womans University, in honor of Professor Yeon-ok Kim's retirement from her long and dedicated teaching career at Ewha. Professor Kim, who has ever encouraged her students to use their hard-earned proficiency in English to make the more human side of Korea better understood to people from other lands, has been the motivating force behind this book and *The Morning Bright,* a collection of Korean folk tales published in honor of the late Professor Kathleen Crane of Ewha Womans University, translated by the same group of her former students. The translators have had invaluable help from the expert copyreading of Mrs. Susan Crowder Han and Prof. John Holstein, who gave the tales appropriate and necessary colloquial bounciness. Thanks are also due to Vice President Shin-won Chu and Ms. Kyoung-hee Uhm of Hollym Publishers, who took the publication of this book with a tiger's boundless courage.

CONTENTS

Preface 7

The Personality of the Korean Tiger

Korean Tiger's Habits 14
Tiger's Attempt to Turn Vegetarian 19
The Love of a Tiger 25
The Loyal Tigress 34

Patron of Filial Piety

Bridegroom Fox and Godfather Tiger 42
A Daughter-in-Law's Devotion 51
The Filial Son Turned Tiger 55
Winter Strawberries 58
Son or Father-in-Law? 61
A Filial Son and a Royal Tiger 66
Brothers to the Last 71

Tiger's Gratitude

A Monument for Brother and Sister 78
The Legend of Hogye Hamlet 82
Tiger and the Snakes 86

The Woodcutter and the Tiger Cub 89
Tiger for a Son 92

Tiger the Matchmaker

The Matchmaking Mountain Spirit 96
The Woodcutter and the Bandit's Foster Daughter 99
Charcoal Burner and Lady Scholar 103

Tiger and Famous Historical Personages

General Kang and the Tigers 112
The Tiger and Sŏ Hwadam 123
The Tiger and Kim Ŭng-sŏ 127
The Tiger and Kwak Chae-u 130
Yi Won-jo's Escape from the Tiger 135

Tiger as Divinities

A Righteous Tiger 144
A Hair from the Tiger's Eyebrow 152

Tips for Catching Tiger

Fighting Tiger with Fire 164
The New Mother and the Insatiable Tiger 167
Fifty-Man Pass 171
Tiger and Juju 174
The Salt Peddler and the Monk 178
Human Tiger Bait 182
Greased Puppy 185

Confrontations with Tiger

The Man with the Chessboard Back 190
How Men Began to Travel with Their Wives 202

The Tiger that Learned to Play the Bugle	206
Tiger Indigestion	208
A Woman's Way	211

Greedy and Stupid Tiger

Tiger Ingrate	220
Tiger and Rabbit	224
Tiger Whiskers	230

Tiger Dung

The Bald Drummer	234
A Face in Exchange for a Son	237

The Personality of the Korean Tiger

Korean Tiger's Habits

An old proverb says there is no tiger in Seoul that does not know Inwang Mountain, and no carp that does not know Kwanggyo Bridge. Indeed, Inwang Mountain, so old now it has just about gone bald, was populated so heavily with tigers that it was known as the home of the tiger. And so folklore abounds in stories about the tigers of Inwang Mountain. There are many other tiger tales, too, set in the high hills and mountains, especially in Kangwon Province. Even now we hear of an occasional sighting there.

Since lions do not exist in Korea, in Korean folk tales it is the tiger who reigns as king of beasts and terrifies all other animals.

Take the cat for instance. The two are in many respects quite similar and, indeed, there are some stories in this collection which tell of how the tiger cub and the cat are sometimes confused. But they are natural enemies of the highest order, like cats and dogs. Tigers hate cats because the cat, as far as the tiger is concerned, is impertinent in the way it dares to imitate the tiger, king of the wilds, in every way, right down to the color of its fur. And so it is said that when a tiger does a cat in, it does not simply chew it up and swallow it in a couple of gulps but tears it to pieces.

The tiger and cat, however, are not the same in every respect. The cat, for instance, can climb trees, whereas the tiger cannot; of course, the tiger would say of itself that it *does* not. So the best thing a person can do to get away from a tiger is run up a tree. Another difference between the two is the way a cat will tuck its tail away when it sits down, which a tiger does not.

The tiger is a very cautious creature. Take, for instance, when it enters its den: it goes in rear end first. This way it can check with its sensitive tail to find out whether anyone is in there.

The tiger, like any other animal attacking a human, will set its hind legs firmly on the ground and raise its front legs. But it is unlike other animals in that, if you can grab it by its waist, from behind, you will be able to constrain its awesome strength.

If you lose your way in the mountains of this country, you do not have to worry too much about the tiger attacking you. It usually has no intention of doing so—if you are virtuous, that is. In fact, it will guide and protect you, lighting up his eyes brightly to brighten your path. When you finally come near your destination, by the way, announce in a loud voice on the hill overlooking your village, "A great personage has come to visit; prepare a warm welcome!" The tiger will then come down with you to the village, take its pick of some hapless dog, pig or other village animal it encounters, and disappear.

Watch out, though, if by some bad stroke of luck you should cross its path in the mountains, because it will take this as a dangerous threat to himself. And, if you are not virtuous, the tiger will not see you as a human but as a dog, and devour you on the spot. How does it know whether you are virtuous or not? The tiger does not act on its own. The mountain spirit inspires it to take whatever action it does.

If you think you are a generally virtuous person but, like most of us, sometimes have your doubts and are not all that confident how the tiger will see you, there are ways to cope with the tiger. Way back in the old days, the elderly would carry a pouch of dried wormwood with them and burn it when they were out in the mountains. The tiger is afraid of fire more than anything else, and cannot stand the thought of its fur being burnt. If you cannot come up with some wormwood, try another trick the people of old used: wear clothing of white rice paper. Just as dogs cannot see snow, tigers are said to be blind to white paper.

The tiger, though, has its own tricks. In the spring young girls will go into the mountains for herbs and green vegetables. If the tiger overhears a girl tell her companion she is thirsty, it will lure her into its clutches by hiding behind a bush or rock and making the sound of running water.

If you are unfortunate enough to be discovered by a tiger while you are sleeping, but fortunate enough to realize, before you panic, that you have been dis-cov ered, just keep lying there. The tiger will not carry you away until it sees you have woken. A tiger will never eat a dead body, human or animal; it does not even keep its catch for the next day's leftovers. Beware, though. The tiger may soak its tail in water and pat your face with it to wake you up.

A genuinely bad person should just stay out of the mountains. If a tiger gets you it will play with you by first grabbing you in its teeth and then suddenly tossing you in the air; if you land to its left, you are safe and it will not eat you. But if you land to its right, you are a goner. It will carry you away on its back to a nice place where it can eat you up in comfort. But even the tiger knows empathy, and will refrain from eating your skull and the bones of your hands and feet. In fact, it will put these on top of a high rock so that your family can find something left of you to give you a proper funeral.

Yes, the tiger does have its soft side. The love it has for its cubs is as strong and tender as that of human parents for their children. When a cub is born the tiger will not eat any domestic animal within an area of 30 *ri** of its cubs, for fear that the owner of the animal might follow the tiger to its cubs.

One other characteristic of the tiger tells us also something of the ox. You can keep a tiger away from your ox by hanging a bell on its neck. That is what country people do, because the tiger fears the bell's ring. Even if you do not have a bell, your ox does not have much to worry about. As we know, a tiger always goes for the neck of its prey when it attacks. It is pretty difficult for a tiger to kill an ox, because the skin on the ox's neck is so tough and rubbery the tiger cannot sink its teeth in.

But a tiger will nevertheless attack an ox on occasion. Your ox will not flee, though; instead it will moo loudly to warn you, and will, in fact, even move closer to you to protect you. Slip your ox from its tether, and it will position you behind itself and do battle with the tiger with all its might. If you shout encouragement your ox will fight until it gores the tiger to death with its horns. But if you just stand there petrified with fear and do not encourage your ox, your ox will take care of you right

---

*Ri : a measure of distance, about one-fourth of a mile.

after it takes care of the tiger. This is because the ox will have become both exceedingly proud of itself and contemptuous of you, its cowardly former master.

Tiger's Attempt to Turn Vegetarian

Long ago an attractive young woman worked in a village wine house. She made wonderful food and was a talented singer and dancer. Naturally, she drew many to the tavern seeking her food and favors.

Then one day she saw a great emptiness in this kind of life, and went off to live in a small hut far out of town. That did not stop the young men from visiting her. Every one that came, though, left without having achieved his goal of gaining her love.

One day in early spring a young man visited her. She showed him the same cool demeanor of indifference that she showed every other man, but he persisted.

"Dear lady, my one wish is to spend my life with you. Why do you have to live this lonely life way out here all by yourself? Let me love and care for you."

His hackneyed line had no effect on the lovely woman, so he swore, with all his heart, "Your coldness does nothing to weaken my resolve. Reject me, ignore me; I will just stay here until you feel my undying love. Till the day I die, if need be."

Just then they heard a low call from outside. The lovesick man's face flushed red with embarrassment, but the woman welcomed whatever it was interrupting the man's courting. She opened the door, and there was a huge tiger crouching at the door.

The young woman was overcome with fear, and nearly fainted. But she was of stout heart, and pulled herself together. "Come in, Tiger."

Tiger strolled in, looking as if he owned the place. The ashen-faced young man with his undying and all-conquering love scrambled out through the side door.

With that she was rid of another one of those boring young men, but how on earth was she going to handle this next visitor? What was she even to say to start the conversation? So she just tried, "Good evening, Tiger. So... What brings you to this shabby shack of mine?"

"Well, young lady," he growled, "this is quite a difficult thing for me to ask you." He looked longingly at her, wiped the saliva from his mouth. "But how about it, would you grant me just one wish?"

Oh no, yet another animal wants me! "What is it? I'll do whatever I can to help," she said in a composed voice which belied her trembling heart.

"Well, you see... We tigers have never eaten vegetables. Not since the days of our forefathers, that is. We eat small animals, as you know. But we feel so sorry for them."

"Why do you eat them then?" The young lady's curiosity got the better of her fear.

"If we don't eat them we'll starve to death! As you know, of course, we certainly aren't starving to death at all—we're doing quite well, in fact. And it's natural that the more tigers you have around the fewer small animals can survive. Some of their kind have already become extinct, you know."

This tiger did not sound like the usual ferocious tiger, but then there were those other stories she had heard.

"And if they go, that's not very good for the tigers who depend on them, is it?" the woman ventured.

"It's not a kind world out there... So," he continued in his gruff voice, "we've decided to change our diet to vegetables, like you humans eat."

"There are lots of vegetables in the mountains. Why come to me?"

"Why come to you?" he roared impatiently. The

young lady's heart all but stopped. "How is one to fix the vegetables without garlic? So you have to be able to eat garlic before you can eat vegetables."

"Then what...what...?"

"What can you do? You can give me some garlic, of course!"

"I... I... But now is when we plant it. I have only a few left for planting. None at all left for eating."

"Come now, just a few? All you have to do is plant a little less."

Fear is one thing. Losing your garlic, though, is quite another. She felt a bolt of courage flow through her. "No, I wish I could, but no."

"Yes. I'm not leaving until you give me some garlic."

"I need that garlic. All of it. I'm very sorry, but no."

"Maybe I'll have to eat you then, instead of vegetables or those poor little animals."

You'll not get my garlic, she swore to herself, no matter what. Then it hit her: This tiger has never tasted vegetables before, and he most certainly hasn't tasted garlic, so how would he even know what garlic looks like? I'll give him some dasheen instead. It not only looks like garlic, it tastes like it too!

She made a great show of fear though, and then relented. "All right. I may starve to death because of this, but wait, I'll get some for you." And she went and got a couple dasheen.

Tiger grabbed them and gobbled them down in the blink of an eye. He gave a small burp, then licked his chops as if those dasheen tasted darn good. "Okay, let's have a few more."

"No. I'll plant the rest and give you plenty next year. In the meantime..."

"In the meantime I'll have a few more." Tiger

growled softly but menacingly.

"Oh, all right. I guess it's better starving to death than getting eaten by a tiger." And she gave him three more dasheen.

He gulped these down as fast as he had the first two. Then, saying he'd be back for more after the harvest, he was off.

The young woman soon planted the garlic she had rescued from Tiger. In the summer she harvested the garlic bulbs and hid them away in a safe place.

Summer turned to autumn, and then, when the fields were covered with a white frost, came the day to harvest the dasheen. And soon after that came Tiger, looking for his garlic.

"I see you haven't starved, young lady," Tiger teased her. "The way you moaned and groaned I thought I'd find a pile of bones here. But you have survived!"

"Barely," she said, and went out to the field to bring Tiger back a few dasheen.

"I've reserved this much for you, Tiger," giving him a basketful. "You're in luck. This year's garlic is better than last year's, quite full and round. Here, try one."

He gulped it down and was so happy he laughed. "Thank you, generous lady! I'll have a few now, and save the rest for winter. And I should be able to eat vegetables beginning next year."

"Absolutely no doubt about it."

Tiger all but inhaled a few more dasheen, wiped his happy chops, and said, "Thank you, dear. And goodbye!"

The young woman watched him leave, a contented smile on her face. "He won't be coming back for garlic anymore. I can live in peace now."

Tiger ate the rest of the "garlic" the young woman

had given him. But alas, he still couldn't manage to get any vegetables down. "My, it seems we're never going to become vegetarians," he moaned. "We'll just have to keep on eating animals, small *and* big. And once they're all gone we might even end up eating each other. Alas, but life is not kind!"

So Tiger began running after his small animals again. And he has remained a carnivore to this day.

The Love of a Tiger

These days there is not even a trace of Howonsa, but long ago this temple was known far and wide for its strange yet beautiful love story.

Way, way back, in the days of the Shilla Dynasty, in the reign of Wonsŏng, there lived a young man named Kim Hyŏn.

At that time Buddhism flourished throughout the country. At the great temple Hŭngnyunsa was a pagoda, and a legend of the time had it that, from the lunar month's eighth day to its full moon on the fifteenth, if you circled the pagoda more than anyone else you would get your wish.

Kim Hyŏn's wish was to become a great man and one day to save his country from some great peril. So one night, the moonlight on his face, he was circling the pagoda, chanting a sutra. The hours passed, the others gave up one by one and went off to their homes, and soon Hyŏn was there alone. The night was deep, and still, as if hushed by a newly fallen snow.

Then Hyŏn saw a silhouette ahead in the bright moonlight, and approached it, slowly, to see what it was. He soon realized that it was the outline of a woman. At first he felt a great fear—it might be a ghost,

some vicious vixen. But then he chided himself. "How can a man who has dedicated himself to save his country shake so at the sight of a woman?"

All was quiet. The silence of the night was broken only by the sound of early morning prayers to Buddha coming from the temple's sanctuary. Hyŏn stood still for a moment, his eyes closed, palms folded, to calm his throbbing heart. When he opened his eyes he could still see the woman's form, shimmering there in the moonlight.

"Is this some evil spirit incarnate come to test my courage and will?" he asked himself. Terrified as he was, he was also curious. He walked faster. He caught up with the woman and, passing her, gave her a sidelong glance. She too raised her eyes a little, and looked at him. Their eyes met, the sparks flew. Then the woman, with her rosy flesh and beautiful face, lowered her head. Hyŏn was so struck by this heavenly apparition that he could not move a limb. It was as if he had turned into a statue of granite.

"Can this be some heavenly goddess? But what kind of desperate wish could a goddess have that she would be circling the pagoda in the middle of the night when everybody else is asleep?" he wondered. His heart pounded with excitement. His fear disappeared, and he began to feel intoxicated with warm desire.

Just then the woman passed out of sight, behind the pagoda. He followed, and as he circled just out of sight, his whole being shuddered with the thought of seeing her once again. He couldn't bear it any longer, and bounded a couple steps ahead. But she was nowhere to be seen.

The next day the image of the woman lingered in Hyŏn's mind all day. Before he went off again to the pagoda he paid special attention to his attire, dressing as if he were going to meet his lover.

The woman was already there, circling the pagoda. When their eyes met again it seemed to Hyŏn that they were exchanging greetings from the deepest depths of their hearts. His head reeled from the shock of love he felt.

The second and then the third day passed, and they finally began to converse. Before long they adored each other.

Finally came the last day of the ritual, the last day they would be able to see each other. The full moon shone quietly on the two young lovers standing at the foot of the pagoda.

"It's the last day," said Hyŏn.

"So it is."

The woman's half-whispered reply saddened Hyŏn. After a while, the sound of Hŭngnyunsa's bell calling the monks to dawn prayers interrupted their bittersweet conversation. They began to walk toward the woods together.

"Lady, though our time together was so short, I will never forget you. Not even till the day I die."

"I feel the same."

"Then please allow me to go with you to your home tonight," said Hyŏn.

This meant a proposal. The woman looked deep into Hyŏn's eyes, and a tear wet her lovely cheek. Soon they were walking together, unaware that they were holding hands.

They came to a small hut. Inside an old woman was waiting for her daughter to return.

"Mother, I've brought a visitor."

"Who?"

The young woman explained what had happened, and then, with her mother's nod, asked Hyŏn inside.

"But daughter dear, your brothers will return soon. What will they say?"

As soon as she finished the words they heard the frightful roar of tigers just outside the hut.

"Hide him, quickly! If he is discovered by your brothers, he's finished. Please, young man, hurry! Hide him in the loft, quick!"

As soon as the young woman got Hyŏn up into the loft three tigers bolted into the room with the speed of lightning and the sound of thunder.

"Mother, what is this smell? It smells like a human. Where did you hide him? I'm hungry!"

"You boys must be crazy. What smell? I can't smell a thing."

"Maybe you can't, but I can. I smell a meal!"

"Nonsense! Besides, it seems you still don't understand how much against killing the Buddha is. If you destroy life you cannot avoid punishment from heaven. Now, enough of your nonsense. Go on, out of here with you all!"

But the tigers looked here and there for their prey. Just then a stern voice from heaven scolded, "You villains will suffer my heavenly wrath if you do not reform and stop your wanton killing!"

At this the tigers trembled and wept, begging for their lives.

"Don't worry," said the young woman. "Please, if you leave here right now I'll take the punishment for you. But, before you go, promise me one thing, that from now on you will never kill another human."

The three swore they would honor their sister's tearful request, and slunk off in dejection, heads bowed and tails between their legs.

When the woman opened the door to the loft, she found Hyŏn in a very sorry state. "So, now you know. I am also a tiger. You must be terrified, poor man! Don't worry, though, I won't harm you. I love you. But now that you know what I am, you cannot possibly love me as before. Well, I was fortunate beyond belief to have been loved by you and return your love. You have given me great happiness, and I must be satisfied with that wonderful gift. If I lived a hundred years I could never forget you. However, I do have to die tomorrow. So please grant me a wish."

"But why on earth would you have to die? You were born an animal, but your virtue can change everything for us. Please, live with me, and don't say anything more about dying."

"No, dear one. It is my destiny. Tomorrow I must die on my brothers' behalf. But if I have to die, I long to die in your arms. Do you know what I was praying for while I was circling the pagoda? I prayed to be born in the next life as a human being. If that wish is granted to me, I will go now without regret."

"Oh my dear, dear lady, don't say that. Tell me this is all untrue. A joke. A dream. You mustn't die!"

"Please, listen. Tomorrow I will turn into a large tiger, and I will go to the marketplace and wreak havoc there. So the King will decree that the person who kills the tiger will be rewarded with money and a high position in the government. You come to the court, then, and announce that you will kill the tiger." With this she put a dagger in his hands.

"Tiger you may be, but I love you. This love of ours is our *karma*. And how could I ever take this life so dear to me for money and position? Never!"

"Please do what I say. This is my fate. And since I must die, I want it to be at your hand."

The very next day a tiger did indeed appear in the marketplace and created an awful havoc. It snapped and snarled and threatened everyone in sight, though it did not attack a single person or carry anyone away into the mountains. And sure enough the government decreed that whoever killed the tiger would be rewarded.

Many young warriors came forward, all eager to show off their skill and valor. Every one of them that got near the ferocious beast, though, was mauled terribly. Then Hyŏn appeared and, his heart breaking, single-handed drove the tiger off toward the woods as his love had bidden him. The tiger and her pursuer left the others far behind.

When they got deep enough into the woods, the tiger turned and faced him. But now it was the beautiful

form of his lady love. "Thank you. I've put you through a lot, and I shall never forget your kindness. Now, dearest, it's time." She waited for him to stab her. "Please, hurry. They're coming."

But Hyŏn could not do it. He could only stand there, numb, speechless. She gazed her last at him with sad yet impatient eyes. And then she snatched the dagger from him and plunged it into her own neck. Hyŏn jumped to grab the dagger, but it was too late. Her rich red blood was already gushing from the wound.

"Please, don't grieve. It is good. We will meet again in the next world. There we can consummate this precious love. But there is one more thing. Gather all that I wounded today, and send them to Hŭngnyunsa, where you will find a balm to cure their wounds. But they must listen to the sound of the temple's bell as you apply the balm. And a temple for me. Please build a temple on this spot, for the repose of my soul..." And she was no more.

Clutching her to his breast, Hyŏn wept the hot bitter tears of absolute despair. But soon the shouts of the hunters and villagers brought him to his senses. When he opened his eyes he found that he was holding not his beloved lady but a tiger, with a dagger in its throat.

The King praised Hyŏn's courageous feat and rewarded him with a huge sum of money and a high position in his court. Hyŏn then found the balm of Hŭngnyunsa and gathered those wounded by the tiger to the temple. As the temple bell sounded in their ears he applied the balm to their wounds. Their wounds were completely cured, and Hyŏn became even more famous throughout the land.

Hyŏn then used the great money he received to build a temple at the spot where his tiger died. And he named the temple Howonsa, Temple of the Tiger's Wish. Through the rest of his life he often visited the temple and prayed for the soul of his beloved, trying to salve his own bitter grief of lost love.

The Loyal Tigress

About two hundred families lived in the peaceful Chŏlla Province village near Mujang. One of these families was a very small one, just a son and his widowed mother.

The son, Chŏng, was known for both his filial piety and his great strength. His father had died when Chŏng was very young, and Chŏng had been taking care of his mother all these years. The kind and caring son took such good care of her, in fact, that he was regarded as a model son by the villagers.

As we know, though, life is not always good to those who are good. One day Chŏng's mother became sick and the illness lingered on and on. Chŏng did everything he could to find a cure for her, but her illness did not leave her.

One day an old monk on his rounds begging alms stopped in front of their house. Instead of going ahead and chanting and knocking out the rhythm on his wood clapper to let them know he was waiting outside, he hesitated. He sensed that there was something different about this home, something not right.

Chŏng saw the monk as he came around from the cow shed. He bowed to the monk, and the monk, as he finished returning the bow, told Chŏng, "Something's wrong here, something very wrong."

"How did you know that? If you know that, you certainly are no common monk. Then maybe you can tell me how I can cure my mother's illness," Chŏng implored.

The monk saw how grieved the good son was over his mother's condition, and responded gravely, "Your father was a warrior, a man of matchless valor and prowess. You know that, of course, better than I. Do you also know what happened after he was released from military service, on the day he went to the market in Mujang?"

"You mean the tiger?"

"On his way home from the market your father decided to take his A-frame off and enjoy a rest in the grove at Yŏnggu Rock. It was already getting dark, and anyone knows the woods are no place to be in the dark."

Yes, Chŏng had heard the story. He had heard it from his mother, who had told it to him repeatedly. And there wasn't a person in the village who did not know the story. His father was resting on Yŏnggu rock when a tiger appeared in a gust of wind. Being a courageous man he did not hesitate to challenge the tiger with his staff. He speared the tiger's eyes one by one, and that was that for the tiger. And the story of his fight and victory spread through the area.

"He beat that tiger all right. Yes, he survived that night. But soon after he caught a strange illness. No one even knew what it was, so no matter how many medicines and cures they tried on him, it was no use. You know why? The mate of the tiger your father killed put a spell on him. Yes, tigers can do that."

"But what has this to do with...?"

"I'm getting to that. The mate that cast that fatal spell on your father has still not had her fill of her desire for revenge. And so she has cast that same spell on your mother. She will eventually kill your mother the same way she killed your father. And she will ultimately get you, too."

"Is there any way out of this?"

"Maybe. But you will need lots of courage. Naturally, the only way to stop that tigress from killing your mother and yourself is to kill her first. The tigress lives behind Yŏnggu Rock." The monk looked deep into Chŏng's eyes, then said, "Bless you, son," and was gone.

This troubled Chŏng to no end. This Yŏnggu Rock tigress was a vicious one, feared far and wide. She often came down to the village and dragged off innocent children and any chicken, pig, or dog that happened to cross its path. The villagers were not safe for a moment, day or night. This all started happening after Chŏng's father killed the tiger at Yŏnggu Rock, so everyone knew that he was the one who started all this.

The magistrate of Mujang decreed that whoever killed the tigress would be given a comfortable government position. The tigress was not brought down, though, and continued to cause such a problem that the magistrate went a step further: he announced that whoever killed the tigress would be given the hand of his daughter in marriage. However, even this was not incentive enough for people who had seen the shredded remains of the tigress' victims. And so now it was all up to Chŏng.

The area near Yŏnggu Rock was thickly wooded, but surrounding the rock was a small clearing. The clearing was crossed by a very narrow path leading to Mujang. On each side of this path were high cliff-like rocks. These would prevent anyone from escaping an attack from the tigress. The tigress lived very well protected in a cave among these rocks. People never travelled this section of the path by themselves; one either went in a large group or did not go at all.

Chŏng knew the danger involved in trying to kill this tigress which had killed so many of his villagers. But he had no other choice: it was either the tiger or his mother. So the day after he talked with the monk he set off, telling no one, with a sharp hook in one hand and a strong net in the other. He also carried a torch, although it was daytime, because he was going to use the tigress' own cave to get her.

He walked along the dangerous path, expecting any moment to be pounced on and torn to shreds. Luckily Chŏng was able to find the tigress' cave before she appeared. He threw the torch into the cave to find out if anything was inside. Not a sound, so he bent down and squeezed himself in through the narrow entrance.

The floor of the cave was strewn with the cracked bones and torn fur of many small animals. Chŏng imagined with a cold shudder the brief, desperate, pitiable battle put up by the victims of this tigress, and shuddered yet again at the thought of his own battle. Then he felt the heat in the tigress' leaf mat. She must have just left. And then again the awful realization of what he was doing struck him. Waiting for a tiger in its own cave.

Chŏng concentrated every nerve in his body on that small entrance. And then he heard the tigress' menacing growl. The entrance darkened with the huge form of this monster, and then there was its thick tail. The

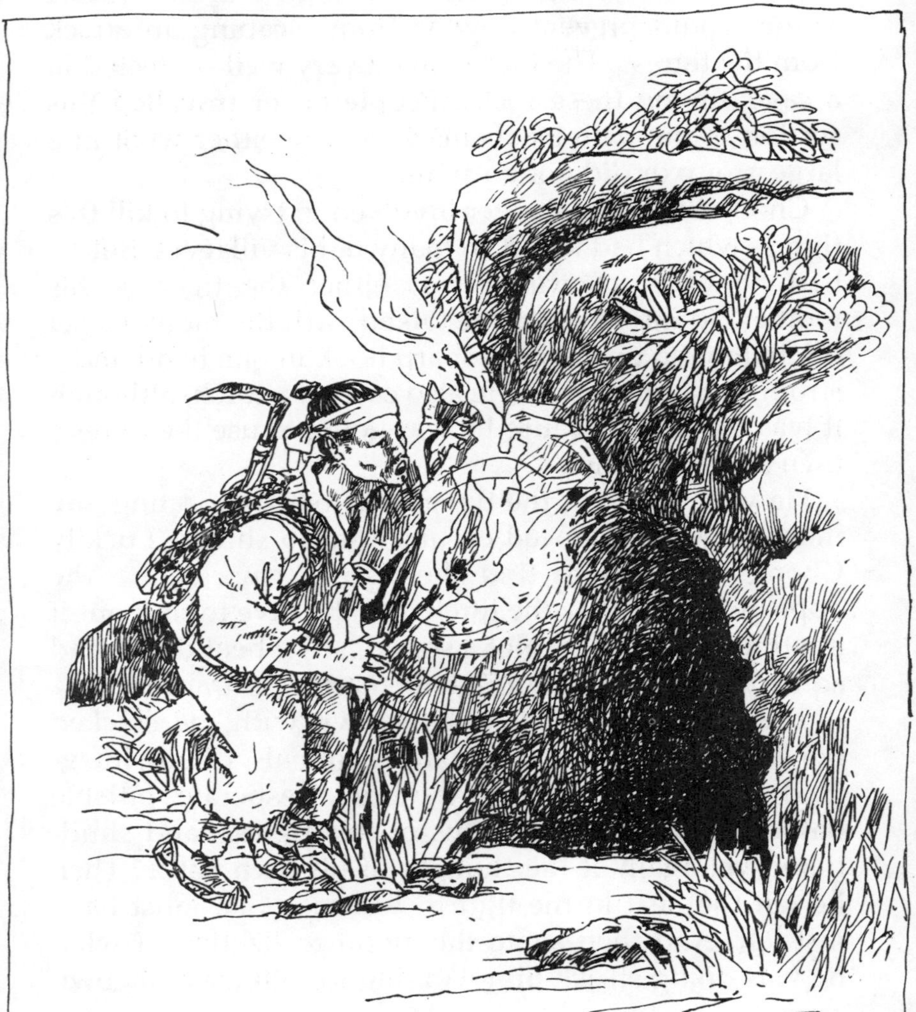

beast started backing rear end first into the cave.

Chŏng quickly spread the net on the ground, and waited. When the tigress' body covered the net, he snatched it up with all his might. The tigress let out a mad howl and a vicious kick. Then he stabbed the furious thing in the back again and again with his hook. As the tigress writhed madly in the small entrance her eyes went big as lanterns and burned with an awesome hate. She tried with every muscle in her powerful body to get back out, but Chŏng was so scared he could not have let go even if he wanted. Then he set her fur on fire with the torch, and kept on stabbing away at her writhing body.

Finally the tigress died. Even after he fully regained his senses Chŏng was so exhausted by the battle and so enervated from the sight of the tigress' bloody carcass that he could only sit and stare vacantly.

He then got up slowly and went back to the village, with no thought of victoriously carrying the tiger with him to show it off. In the village he told the villagers to go back and get the tiger, but how could anyone believe that a single human had killed that demon tigress? Finally, though, a group of them did go to the cave and witness the results of the battle.

Chŏng thought his happiness was complete when his mother suddenly recovered. But it was not over for him yet. The magistrate, when the villagers reported the story to him, kept his promise and made him an official in his office. And, to make Chŏng's life happy ever after, the magistrate's beautiful daughter became his wife.

Patron of Filial Piety

Bridegroom Fox and Godfather Tiger

In the seventeenth century, around the middle of the Chosŏn dynasty, there lived a country official in a small village in Hwanghae Province. The man was by nature good and gentle, and he got along well with his neighbors. He had two good and loving children, Nan-hyang, 18, and Su-dong, 15.

One day the official was robbed of the enormous sum of 1,000 *nyang**. What made this such a calamity was that it was not his money but government funds which he had been entrusted with. The law of the period was harsh, and stipulated that anyone who embezzled public funds would pay for it with his life.

The man was poor, and he had no way of restoring the money. And he had neither relatives nor friends who had enough money to help him. So there was nothing he and his family could do but sit there and worry and wait and sigh till the day came for him to part with his head.

On the day before his sentence was to be carried out he was lying on his mat despondent, helpless. The sun

---

*Nyang: an old Korean coin.

was setting, the day getting darker, and life was moving closer and closer to the next day, when he was to be executed. Then a call came from outside the front gate. "May I speak to the master of the house?"

Nan-hyang and Su-dong were naturally not in a sociable mood, and they did not want to let in any strangers. But they went out to the gate. "We've had a great misfortune here. We're sorry, but could you come back some other time?"

"Let the man in, children. He hasn't come all this way for nothing." And the two showed the stranger into their father's room.

"I'll get straight to the point then. My young master has sent me to tell you that he wants to save your life. No one, he says, should have to lose such a precious thing as his life for a mere 1,000 *nyang*. He sincerely wants to help you."

The despondent father heard this with a surge of hope. He asked imploringly, "Is he really going to help me? Would he spend so much money on someone he doesn't even know? You are not having some cruel sport with us, are you?"

"Certainly not. There is one small condition, though. I'm sure you'll find no problem with it. This daughter of yours, she is very attractive, and she is also at the age to marry. She would make a very good match for my master. That is all he wants, her hand in marriage."

Hearing this the girl's father heaved a sigh. He was suspicious of this incredulous offer from the very beginning, and now his suspicions proved right. No, even if it would lengthen his time on earth, how could he ever give his beloved daughter to a total stranger? Sell his daughter? "I cannot accept your master's offer. My life is precious to me, but to force my daughter into marriage for money...."

His daughter had been eavesdropping on their conversation and, when she heard her father refuse the offer that would save his life, she stepped into the room and said with great determination, "Father dear, please don't worry. It's time that I marry anyway, and I might as well marry the man who can save your life. Please allow me to accept the gentleman's offer."

"No. Absolutely not. I'd rather lose my head to the executioner than lose my daughter to a man who would buy her."

Nan-hyang's mind, though, was set, and she was going to give herself to the man who would save her father. No one could weaken her resolve. So at last, with great reluctance, her father consented.

The messenger smiled. "I will bring the money tonight, before it's too late. In the meanwhile, please get everything ready for the wedding."

Soon after he left porters arrived carrying great chests bulging with money. After the porters left Nan-hyang wondered, as the hours ticked away, what her new husband would be like. She could hardly stand the suspense and her heart was throbbing with all kinds of possibilities when a handsome, brightly dressed young man appeared. His appearance aroused waves of excitement in her. And she could not understand how everything was happening, how the wedding was being readied, so quickly after it was agreed to.

As soon as the wedding was over, though, the bridegroom suddenly said that he had to hurry off to take care of some urgent matter at home. Nan-hyang's family was sorely disappointed at this, because they were expecting Nan-hyang and her new husband to stay with them for a few days, as was the custom in those days.

Su-dong could not stand parting with his beloved sister so abruptly, so just as soon as the new couple mounted their horses and left, he jumped on another horse and followed. But then the bridegroom somehow sped his wife and himself along so quickly that it was all Su-dong could do to keep them in sight. Even this became impossible soon, and he eventually lost them. He could not even tell which direction they disappeared in. So all he could do was give up and go back home.

While Su-dong was making his lonely way back, Nan-hyang found herself in a seemingly limitless cavern, which was lined with streets with huge rich houses. She was led by her bridegroom to the biggest of these. It was already astir with activity, and many people came up and welcomed her to her new family. Though she was anxious and missed her family back home, all the brightness and friendliness helped to make her start feeling a little better.

She obediently did as she was directed by her new family. She sat with her new husband at the head of the table, let her husband embrace her in front of everyone, and did not try to stop her husband from drinking so much and carousing around. In fact, the festive mood was catching, and she even began to join in the merriment. The whole house rang with song and laughter and glowed with the sights of happy people making merry.

Then, in the midst of all this boisterous banquet, a whirlwind sprang up with the sound of thunder. And out of this whirlwind, lo and behold, came an old man with long white hair. And then... Everyone was gone, everyone except Nan-hyang and the old man.

Nan-hyang, of course, was completely bewildered. Had she been bewitched by some evil spirit? She trembled in the presence of the old man who had made everything stop so suddenly, and almost fainted when the old man approached her.

"This is no place for you. Come on, we're getting out of here. Get on my back."

With this Nan-hyang did faint, and so the old man put her on his back himself and took off. When she came to, she was in a completely different land, one she had never seen before. She looked around, rubbed her eyes, trying to make sense out of all this. All she could see was a deserted old house, and she shook her head to get rid of this bad dream. Then she heard the old man's voice again.

"I am a tiger. Old, a hundred years old. Don't worry, though, this tiger's not going to hurt you, dear. In fact, I have saved you from being hurt. Your bridegroom is a fox, a thousand-year-old fox. He disguises himself as a handsome young man and casts a spell on young maidens like yourself, makes them his bride, and then devours them. It's impossible to count the number of young lasses he's already done in like that. I want to stop him, to make him pay for his cruelty, but I can't. I'm ashamed to say I have never been able to catch him, no matter how hard I have tried.

"I was passing by on my way home from the hunt when I saw you there in the midst of that spell he created. If I hadn't seen you there, you would not be alive now to hear this story. Now don't worry, you are safe. And soon you will be back home with your loved ones."

As soon as he finished, he leaped in the air and turned a somersault. And when he landed, he was a tiger.

Nan-hyang stayed there with the tiger for a few years, so that he could protect her from the fox. During the day she dried the hides of the animals he had caught and in the evening she cooked their meat.

One afternoon, while Nan-hyang was washing her clothes, she heard an odd sound coming from a ditch nearby. She listened carefully, and soon recognized a man's voice. She was so frightened she just kept on working, a lot harder now, not even daring to look out of the corner of her eye. Then, after a while of this, it became so unbearable she turned toward the sound, expecting to see the fox. It wasn't a fox, though, it was her bridegroom. Now what was she ever to do?

"Nan-hyang, it's me, your husband. Why do you just stand there? Come, follow me! That clever old devil tricked you—he's a hundred-year-old tiger, and one of these days... You'll get into a lot of trouble if you don't

48 Tiger, Burning Bright

run away with me right now!" said her husband.

But at the very moment the young man was going to grab her hand and pull her away with him, the tiger returned from his hunt. The young man tried to flee, but the tiger was quicker and pounced on the bridegroom. With a painful cry the young man died, and his dead body turned into a fox with nine tails.

The tired tiger panted, and then sighed with relief. "Well, demon, that's it for you. I've finally got you." Then he turned on Nan-hyang. "How foolish of you to stand there and let him try to talk you into following him. The only thing you would have got from that was death. Keep your guard up in this life, dear."

After dinner the tiger announced, "Well, the fox is dead. You won't be needing me anymore to protect you. Come, you're going home. Up on my back!"

This time she did not hesitate, and she was on his back in the blink of an eye. They literally flew over the hilly roads winding through the deep mountains, the cool wind tickling Nan-hyang's cheeks and the train of her long skirt fluttering out in back.

And then, almost before she knew it, the tiger came to a stop in front of her old home.

"Well, lass, here you are. This is where you get off. Now go on inside and show yourself to your parents."

Nan-hyang was torn with emotions tugging in different ways. She wanted so much to return to her family, but she also loved the tiger who had saved her life twice and been so kind to her. "Go on," said the tiger, "I'll wait to see that everything's okay."

So she could put off parting for a while at least. Then she took a deep breath and dashed into the yard of her old home, calling to her mother.

A gaunt, haggard woman looked out the door. "Who

are you, girl? Your mother is not here. I'm here all by myself."

"Mother, it's me! Nan-hyang. I'm back!"

"But..."

"That was an old fox that I was sold to, not a real man..."

"What are you saying, girl? My daughter married a rich man, and then...died. Now, don't bring back that grief to me."

"Mother, don't you recognize me? I'm that very same daughter you lost years ago." She burst into tears.

"Well I do believe... Are you really my Nan-hyang? Nan-hyang, it is you! You're back, alive!" And she clutched her daughter to her bosom.

The two wept tears of joy. And then Nan-hyang said through her tears, "Come, Mother, we must prepare a big pot of rice and pork and a huge beef stew for my hungry friend."

"But you have to tell me what happened. Of course we'll feed your friend, we'll have the biggest celebration ever. But let's take our time about it as you tell me what has been going on with you all these years."

"Well, this is how it all happened. My bridegroom..." And Nan-hyang told her the whole story. "And so you see, Mother, without Tiger, who knows what could have happened to me? And now we must treat him as well as we know how, to show him our thanks."

So they fed Tiger and entertained him. And soon it was all over. Tiger thanked the two for their kindness and was gone, just like that.

A Daughter-in-Law's Devotion

A long, long time ago a seventy-year-old man and his son, a twenty-year-old woodcutter, lived together in a remote valley. They managed one way or another to eke out a scanty living, but, because they were so poor, the son could not even think of finding a wife for himself. Who would want to marry into a life of such poverty? The father and son were quite lonely, because they had no friends way out there in the middle of nowhere.

Finally they were able to find a woman of marrying age from a family as poor as they were. This marriage did not help the family in any way out of their poverty, but the three loved each other and found they could rely on each other, so they were happy.

This did not last long, though. Just one year after they were married the son fell ill and died. So now the young bride was a widow, burdened not only with making a living for herself but also with taking care of an aged and sickly father-in-law who needed her constant care. The old man felt terribly sorry about this, and he kept asking her to forget about him and marry again. His daughter-in-law, though, never even gave a thought to leaving him in his condition.

At the same time her own parents were also urging

her to marry again. And then one day she got a message that her mother was seriously ill. The young girl, of course, had to visit her. But she would have to leave her father-in-law for quite a while, because her family lived in a village far away. So she prepared as much food as she could for her father-in-law to tide him over during her absence. And then she left with an anxious, heavy heart.

There was no other way to get to her family's village than by foot. After several miles of trudging over those country paths in her straw shoes her feet were blistered and swollen, but she kept on, slow but steady. The slower she walked, the quicker her heart beat with the ever-increasing exertion. And she began to fret whether she would be able to make it to her mother.

Then out of the blue a tiger appeared in her path. She was scared out of her wits and closed her eyes as hard as she could, expecting any second that she would be gobbled down by this huge beast. But nothing happened. So she opened her eyes and saw that the tiger was bending, almost bowing, indicating that she should get on its back. She had already given up her life for lost, so she did as the tiger wanted. As soon as she got up on the tiger's back, they were off like lightning.

After an hour or so of their mad dash the tiger reared to a stop. And there they were, already in front of her parents' home. She did what she could to thank the tiger, thanked whichever of the spirits had made it possible to see her sick mother, and ran into the house.

Her mother greeted her with a leering grin. "So here you are, sweetie. Come to your mother." The young widow realized now that she had been tricked by some evil spirit into making this trip. Yet this was her own mother. But no, it wasn't. What had happened to her mother then? She didn't know, but she did know that she would have to get out of there and back to her father-in-law as fast as possible.

So she started on her way back, with an even heavier heart. The young widow now grieved for not only her lost husband and her sick father-in-law, but also for her mother. In a deep valley, as she was wondering how to handle all this sorrow, the tiger appeared again. She climbed on its back and it shot away with her like an arrow. And she was back home the same day she had left.

She found that the old man, pining away at losing his beloved daughter-in-law and feeling completely abandoned, had not even touched his food. But now he was overwhelmed with happiness to see her back with him.

That night, on the way back to his mountain but still near the young widow's home, the tiger fell into a pit trap that a hunter had dug. She heard the tiger's frantic howls and guessed it was her tiger, so she hurried out and found her tiger and the hunter. She told the hunter how the tiger had helped her and begged him to let her friend go. But the man was interested only in skinning the tiger and selling its hide, and would not listen.

The young widow did the only thing she could do. She jumped into the pit and told the man to kill her instead of her tiger. The man looked at the tiger and saw those two big eyes pleading for mercy. He was moved by the young widow's loyalty and sense of obligation to the tiger, and finally relented. He helped them both out of the pit and sent them on their way.

Thanks to the tiger and the hunter, then, the young widow was able to care for her father-in-law, keeping him comfortable and happy until the day he died.

The Filial Son Turned Tiger

During the reign of King Kojong, towards the end of the last century, in a small village with the name of Tonggunŭng, there lived a man who was fervently devoted to his mother.

One day his mother was stricken with a fatal disease, and the man fretted endlessly trying to discover some way to save her before it was too late. He spent all his time and energy and money trying to find the right medicine, but alas, all his efforts were in vain.

Then one day he heard that the only thing that would cure his mother was for her to eat one hundred dogs. But how could he ever catch a hundred dogs! Two or three dogs, even a few dogs maybe, but a hundred! Only a tiger could catch a hundred dogs.

And so he found the solution to his dilemma. Eventually, with his great filial determination, he was able to find a magic spell which he used to turn himself into a tiger. Every night he chanted this spell and went out for a few dogs. Then, after his hunt was over, he would chant the spell which turned him back into a human being.

After a few of these late-night hunts he had soon caught all the dogs in his village. But he still didn't have

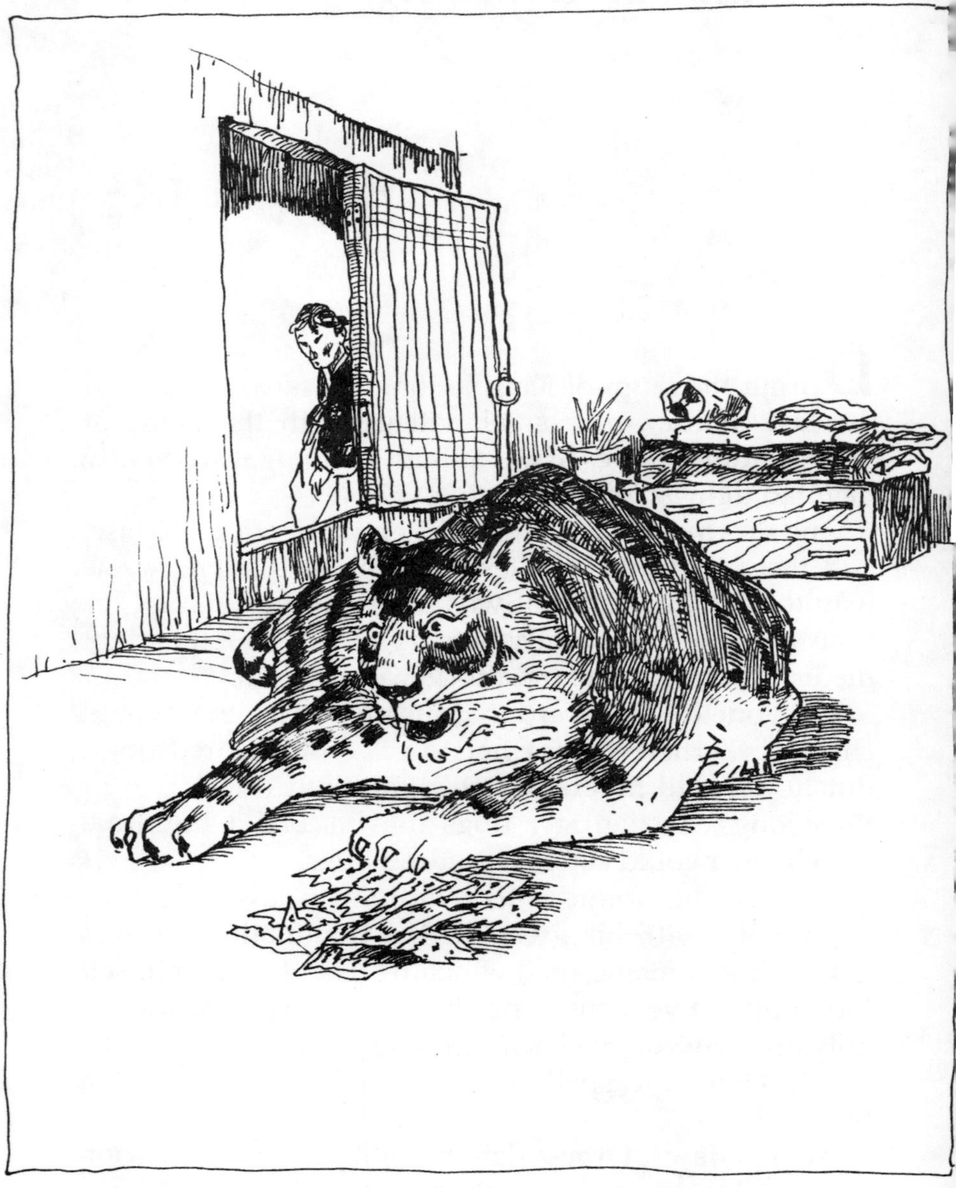

anywhere near the hundred dogs his mother needed. So he started raiding the neighboring villages.

Meanwhile, his wife had become disgusted with his nocturnal doings. After a few more nights of it she got so furious with the whole thing that she tore up the paper on which he had written the spell. When he came back from his raid that night he found his spell torn to shreds and scattered all over the floor. Try as he might, he could not piece the spell back together again.

So the tiger went into a beastly rage, killing his mother, then his wife and son. Then, because his wife had done this to him and her maiden name was Chŏng, he started calling himself Tiger Chŏng. Still in a rage, he attacked the village, this time not looking for dogs but for people with the family name of Chŏng. The village, and then the surrounding villages, went into a panic. It was said that this huge beast had such a big mouth it could hold the heads of five or six people at a time.

At last the government offered an award for the capture of the fierce tiger. There were lots of Chŏngs in this area, and the prize was a handsome one, so a great many banded together and finally proved to be too much for the tiger. He was finally hunted down.

This is why the tiger is said to this day to have the quality of filial devotion.

Winter Strawberries

In a small village there once lived a man who wanted desperately to have a son. He wanted this so desperately, of course, because after many years of marriage he and his wife were childless. The distraught man walked around with a perpetually forlorn look on his face.

Then one day his wife finally did present him with a son. The couple loved the child dearly. Everyone, in fact, loved the child, because this child did everything better than anyone else, was wise and had good judgement, and was never boastful. Theirs was truly a happy family.

But this kind of happiness cannot go on forever, and when the boy was five his father died. So now his mother was all that he had in life. Despite their hard life the boy remained a thoughtful, obedient and devoted son, and his mother took great pride in him.

As the years passed, though, his aging mother became senile and began to suffer from all kinds of illnesses. Day in and day out her son looked for a medicine to help her recover, but nothing worked.

Then one cold winter day with icy wind and deep snow his mother got a craving for strawberries. Strawberries, of course, were not in season, but she wanted strawberries so bad that her son could not ignore her pleas. In her condition she could not know how distraught this impossible request made her son.

He remembered the old saying, "True devotion can move heaven." And he thought to himself that, if his mother needed strawberries this badly, they must be somewhere, even in the middle of winter in this heavy snow and biting cold. And he went out to find them.

He wandered from place to place till he was completely exhausted. He was just on the verge of questioning that old saying when a striped tiger appeared. This tiger motioned for him to get on its back and the son, because he was so obsessed with finding some strawberries, fearlessly jumped on the tiger's back. The next thing he knew, he was in a land of summer and lovely flowers and gorgeous birds. And there, right in front of him, was an old man waiting for him.

The son told this man his story. Then the man said, "You certainly are a devoted son! And you certainly impress me with your single-minded determination. So, you want strawberries, do you? Well, there's a field right over there with as many luscious strawberries as you can imagine," and he pointed to a field nearby. "Go on, pick as many as you wish."

The son ran to the field and filled a basket with enough strawberries to keep his mother happy for many days. He was in such a hurry to get back home that he forgot to make a proper good-bye. The old man understood though, and smiled as he saw this good son going back to his mother.

Before the son got very far there was the tiger again, waiting for him. He hopped on the tiger and was back home before he could even tell the tiger where he wanted to go.

His mother ate the strawberries. They not only tasted good, they also helped her regain her health. And this was all thanks to the kind strawberry tiger.

Son or Father-in-Law?

At the edge of a tiny hamlet near Inje in Kangwon Province stands a stone monument to the mountain spirit. It is quite a nuisance to the farmers there, but they have never given a thought to removing it. They know its story.

Deep in the Sŏrak Mountains, around the end of the sixteenth century, lived a woman named Tolle. In her family was her husband, his father, and their son of three years. Like the others in their hamlet they made their living by searching the mountains for medicinal herbs and selling these herbs in the market many miles away. It was a hard life climbing up and down range after range of these steep mountains. Tolle was happy, though, because she got such joy watching her son grow.

As for her father-in-law, the old man did nothing but drink day in and day out. Tolle did not complain, however; she loved him and did her best to care for him. He was a good man, and besides, he was the father of her husband. Filial devotion was his due. So Tolle and her husband worked hard to gather as many herbs as they could, to give themselves a better life and to keep the old man in wine.

One afternoon Tolle's husband was getting ready to leave for the market to dispose of the herbs they had gathered. It would take him more than a week there and back and another three or four days to trade his goods for fabric, salt and other necessities. As concerned as he was about the heavy pack on his back and the dangers of the long journey ahead of him, he did not forget to remind Tolle to take good care of their father while he was gone. And then he was off.

The next day, after a difficult sleep, Tolle's father mentioned that he was not feeling well, and said he would go to his friend's in the hope that this would cheer him up. Tolle knew that this refresher he was thinking of was not so much the game of Go that he would have with his friend but that wonderful rice brew that his friend always offered. When he left, his ears were reverberating with Tolle's loving admonishments. "Father, please don't stay too long. Don't drink too much! Those mountain trails..."

Night fell, and still the old man had not returned. Already their son was fast asleep, and the crescent moon hung over the western hill. Tolle was anxious and felt she ought to go out looking for the old man, but she did not want to leave her son alone and certainly did not like the idea of going out into the dark alone. After a while, though, she knew she had to go, so she made a torch and went out into the night.

The path was treacherous in the weak light of the torch, and she stumbled a few times along the way. Then all of a sudden she was confronted by two huge lights, and then the menacing roar of a beast. A tiger! Tolle's knees buckled and she dropped to the ground in a faint.

When she came to, she picked up her torch and

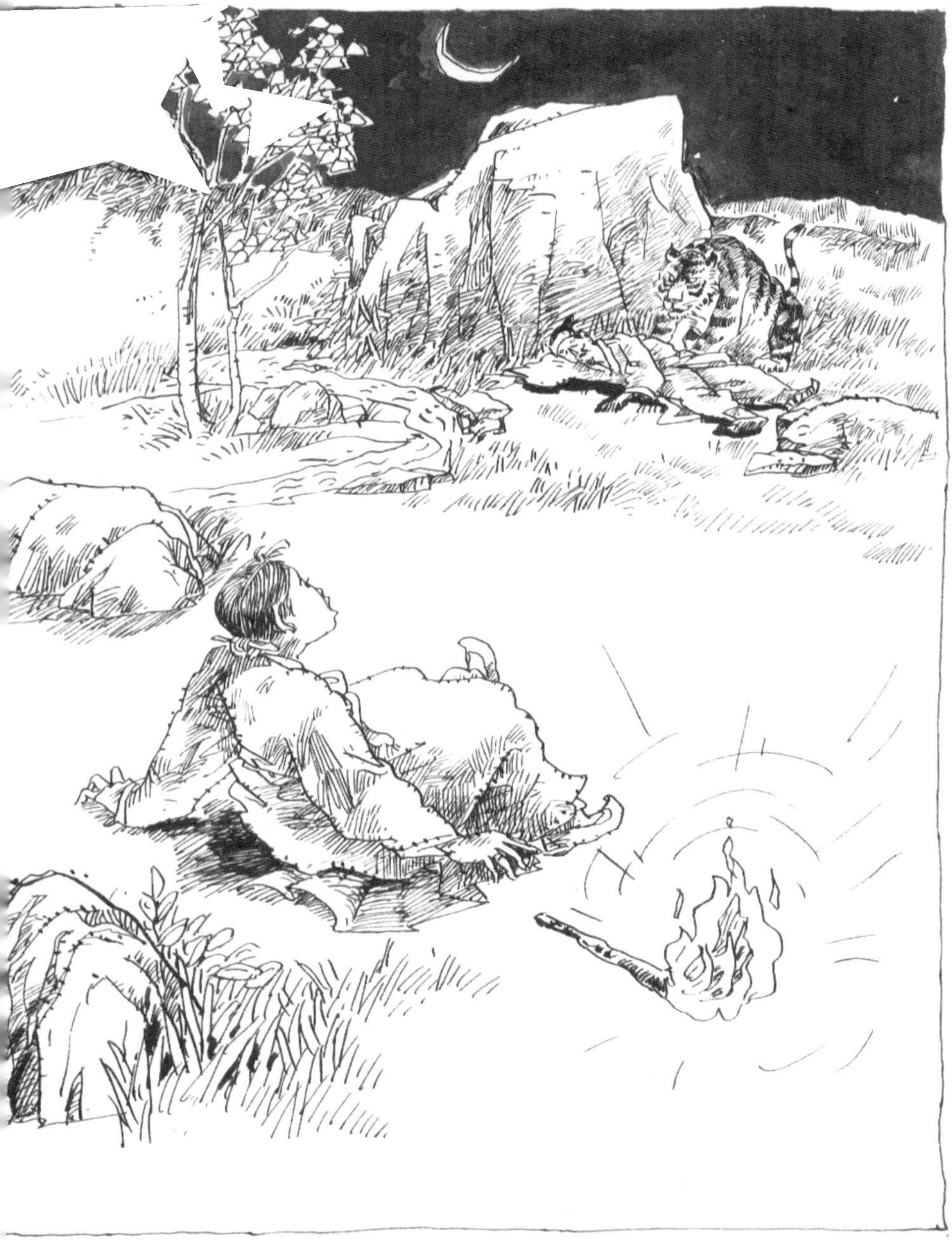

looked around. There was the body of a man, and looming over the body was a tiger as big as a house. Then she recognized the man—her father-in-law! Tolle was petrified with fear and could not move a step, and even if she could she knew she would not be able to leave the old man to the tiger. But she could not fight the tiger, either. So she prayed to the mountain spirit. "Please help my poor father-in-law."

The tiger menaced with another growl. She would have to do better than this. She realized then that she would have to offer something really precious if her father-in-law were to be saved. So she offered the most precious thing in her life. "Take my son instead. I would gladly offer myself, but without me, and with my husband gone, there would be no one to look after the old man."

Right away the tiger picked up the old man in its mouth and arched its back, signaling Tolle to climb up. As soon as she was on the tiger's back, it sped off to their home. When they got there Tolle collapsed under the heavy grief of having to give up her son.

When she opened her eyes again, there was her father-in-law, sleeping. Sure enough, her son was nowhere to be found.

The next day the old man asked where his grandson was. Tolle told him he was at a relative's house. She would tell her husband the truth, though, the whole story. And then she would kill herself.

In a few days her husband returned. He was moved by his wife's story and tried hard to console her. How, though, could the woman be consoled? Only death could stop such pain.

Just then, they heard a knock at the door. When they opened it they saw an old man with long white hair, and in front of the man was their son.

"I am the tiger you met in the mountains. I was sent by the mountain spirit to test your love and devotion to your father-in-law. You have impressed the mountain spirit, and you have impressed me. And so I now give you back your son."

And that is why the farmers may grumble now and then at the monument, but would not think of doing anything about it.

A Filial Son and a Royal Tiger

Way back over two hundred and sixty years ago a young man named Pak lived with his foster mother. The son was so devoted to his mother that he won the admiration of all who knew him.

Pak also excelled in his studies, and passed the higher civil service examination. Mother and son were very happy at this feat, but then, in the midst of their great joy, fate struck its cruel blow. Pak's foster mother died suddenly and left him all alone. Even though he was a young man now, he wept like a child. Indeed, his grief was the awful sort that only tears can begin to express.

Not a day passed that he did not get up before the first cock crowed and walk almost thirty *ri* to his mother's grave, from his house in the center of Seoul into the hills surrounding the city. He even had a hut built near the grave so he could watch over his mother's grave. And every day, after visiting her grave, he would walk back to Seoul, at the break of dawn, to carry out his duties in his government office.

One day on his way to his mother's grave, when he had got into the hills, a huge tiger appeared before him. He was stunned, and froze in his tracks. So it was all up for him now. Pak was not all that afraid to die, though.

He was not so frightened as he was saddened at the realization that he would not be able to tend his mother's grave anymore. And he would not be able to commemorate this or any other anniversary of his mother's death. Having no one to remember her would mean that her soul could not rest in peace.

So he calmly told the tiger, "I guess you have been sent here because I have not been as faithful to my mother as I should. Do as you will. I know you are king of the beasts, and can devour me in the blink of an eye. I also know, though, that you are intelligent, and should know right from wrong. If you think it is right for me to die before I can commemorate the first anniversary of my mother's death, go ahead."

Pak closed his eyes and waited quietly for the tiger to pounce, but it showed no sign of attack. Pak kept on waiting calmly, and then finally heard the swish of the tiger's tail wagging over its back. He opened his eyes and saw the tiger just standing there, watching with an expectant look. At first Pak thought that the tiger was trying to hypnotize him for some devious purpose, but he then realized that the tiger might be signaling him to get on his back. "Is that what you want, then, for me to climb up?"

The tiger blinked his eyes and nodded. So Pak climbed on the tiger's back, and off they sped to his mother's grave. Pak got off and patted the tiger to show his thanks.

Even after Pak finished the service to his mother the tiger was waiting there for him. So he climbed back on and the tiger took him all the way back to the outskirts of the city. Then it bowed three times and disappeared into the thick forest. Was this all a dream? Could this be real?

68 *Tiger, Burning Bright*

On the following day, though, the tiger was there again waiting for Pak. And for four months it showed up every day without fail.

Then one day the tiger was not there waiting. Pak was sorry it did not show, because they had become quite good friends. He waited a while, then sadly shrugged and kept on walking to his mother's grave. Then, as he entered the hills, he came upon several hunters with three tigers trapped in a net. Pak suspected that this explained why his tiger had not shown up that morning, and rushed up to them. Sure enough, there was his tiger, moaning sadly. Pak explained to the hunters that one of the tigers was his, but the hunters protested.

"Finders keepers. Anyway, how can you explain such a silly notion that you own a tiger?"

"I don't own it. It just... Well, you know he just... Anyway, I can prove it's mine. It wags its tail whenever it sees me. Look."

The tiger was indeed looking right at Pak, and wagging its tail. So the hunters released the tiger, and watched the two walk off together.

Soon the news spread far and wide. Even the King heard the story and was deeply impressed by Pak's devotion to his mother. So the King offered him ten *ri* of land surrounding his mother's grave and gave him a high position in the court.

Pak's tiger continued to show up every day. The grave keeper told Pak that the tiger even guarded the grave against wolves and foxes.

Pak continued working hard and faithfully for his King, and finally rose to the rank of minister. When he died, at the age of forty-seven, the country gave him a funeral almost as big as they would for royalty. And the government honored him with a memorial gate in recognition of his filial devotion.

After the funeral the corpse of a tiger was found near Pak's grave. The government honored the tiger by burying it at the foot of its friend's grave. They also built a shrine for the faithful tiger, and posthumously christened the tiger "Royal Tiger."

Brothers to the Last

Once upon a time an old woman and her son lived in a small hut deep in the mountains.

One late night the boy was on his way home after attending to something in the village far away. When he came to the pass on the high hill before his home he found a tiger blocking his path, glaring angrily at him. The son fought to keep his composure, though, and feigned happiness at meeting the tiger.

"Elder brother, it's you! At last!"

The tiger liked this, and responded with a smile. The boy continued, "Now that we're finally back together again, I suppose you'd like to hear how we were separated. Mother tells me that when you were born as a tiger they didn't know what to do, what with the neighbors and all. So father had no choice but to take you deep into the mountains and let you fend for yourself. Both father and mother took it very hard for a long time after that, and never really did forgive themselves. But now you are back, and I'm so awfully glad to meet you."

The tiger nodded his head, showing he understood everything the boy was telling him, then approached the boy. The boy reached up and patted his new brother on the shoulder. "So, let's hurry back and tell mother the good news."

The boy was still scared, but he did not show it. When they reached home, he told the tiger to wait outside while he went in and prepared their mother for the shock.

His mother gave him a big smile of relief when he came in. "You're back, safe and sound!"

"Mother, listen to me, carefully. There is a tiger outside."

His mother almost passed out. "What are you...! My heavens, what should we do?"

"I brought the tiger back with me," he said in a soothing voice, trying to calm her. And he told her everything he had told the tiger. "So please, try to look happy, not like this, like you've seen a ghost. He's your son, you know, whom you haven't seen for years and years. Give him a nice big welcome." But she was still upset, and was sure she would not be able to utter a word. "Don't worry, mother. Do exactly as I asked, and everything will work out fine." And he went out to bring the tiger in.

"Come in brother, come in! You'll see mother is having a hard time recovering from this great news. But she'll get over it. Do come in."

Slowly the tiger walked in, and looked at the woman. When she saw the tiger she did what she had been told to do.

"Oh my dear! My son! My long lost son! You wouldn't believe how I've missed you all these years. And now you're back home with us. Oh, welcome back!"

She was very good, and the tiger believed every word. He said, through his tears, "I have been such a neglectful son to you, but believe me, I didn't know. Please forgive me. From now on I'll take good care of you."

Late the next night the creaking of the wood gate woke the boy from his sleep. He got up and went outside to see who it was. It was the tiger, with a wild boar in its mouth.

"Come in, brother! Thank you!"

So the tiger walked on in. By this time the mother had got up to see what was going on. "Ah, good, you're back! Come, you must be starved," and she offered to cook up a meal of the boar and everything she could find in the house.

"Thank you, but I really can't eat that other stuff. I eat only meat, and I don't cook it. Anyway, the boar is for you and little brother here. Be sure to let it boil at least a couple hours. I hope you like it... Mother."

And the tiger called her Mother from that day on. The woman lost her fear of her new son, and even came to be very fond of him.

The tiger visited whenever he could, and at every visit he came loaded down with meat and firewood. Mother and son never lacked for the sublime comfort that food and warmth can give. Whenever the tiger appeared the two welcomed him gladly, and they soon forgot that the tiger was not really a member of the family. And so peaceful, happy days passed into months, and happy months passed into years.

One day the mother was taken seriously ill. Her son was terribly worried, because nothing he could do would make her feel better. So he went out searching the mountains to find the tiger and tell him the bad news. He spent so much time climbing up and down those steep mountain trails that he exhausted himself. He decided to rest a while on a large, flat rock, and was soon fast asleep. He dreamed that hosts of fairies were coming down from heaven, riding colorful clouds. One of them touched his head and said, "Wake up, and go back home now."

He woke up in a cold sweat. The night was pitch black and he felt awfully lonely. Then, to his surprise, he saw a tiger walking toward him, a wild boar in its mouth. He was relieved to find that the tiger was none other than his brother. "Brother, my brother Tiger!"

"What are you doing out at such a late hour so deep in the mountains? Don't you know how dangerous it is?"

"Mother's sick, very sick. I've been looking all over for you."

"Let's get back, quick!"

The man jumped on the tiger's back and the tiger raced home, very worried. As soon as they arrived they rushed in to their mother.

"Mother, I'm back," said the Tiger. "What's wrong? How can I help...?"

But what, after all, could a tiger do? He could not cool her forehead, nor massage her back, nor go to the village for medicine. All he could do was worry. And worry. His brother went down to the village for some medicine, but returned empty-handed.

Days passed. The long nights wore on. And the mother's health deteriorated alarmingly. There was almost no hope left now. The tiger could not stand it any longer, and went down to the village and searched from house to house for some medicine. The mere sight of the tiger, of course, scared the daylights out of the village people and their animals, and there was quite a commotion.

So the tiger returned home. His brother, tears streaming down his cheeks, met him at the front door. "She's gone."

The tiger flopped down and wept. Its utterly despondent groans reverberated through the mountains, and the heavens seemed about to come crashing down. The people in the villages for miles around heard the mournful wailing and feared that a great catastrophe was about to befall them.

The young man made mourning garb for himself and the tiger. He put his on and went down to the village, telling his neighbors of his mother's death and asking them to help with the funeral. Everyone was sympathetic and, before long, showed up at his house with a casket. Just then the tiger opened the front door, though, and they all fled, falling over themselves in their terror. The young man shouted to them to come back, there was nothing to fear, but they were not about to stop and listen.

So the two brothers were left to carry the casket themselves. It was too clumsy, though, so the tiger just took their mother's body in his mouth. They gave her a simple funeral on a sunny spot on the mountain, and marked the grave with a simple plank.

Without their neighbors to mourn with them it was all the harder to bear their grief. They just sat there and wept their hearts out.

After a while the young man, tears all spent, finally stopped weeping. He put his hand around the tiger's shoulder and said, "Come on, stop now. We'd better get on home."

The tiger could not stop his tears, though. Even after almost a hundred days had passed he was still weeping inconsolably. This exhausted him, and he became so weak that he could not move a muscle. Since he had no thought of food, he began to starve, and soon he became sick.

His brother went to the villagers for some medicine to help the tiger. But they turned their backs on him, insulted him, and some even beat him or threw things at him to chase him off. So he returned home, body bruised and spirit beaten. There was no way he could help his brother.

His tiger brother became weaker and weaker, and finally, one day, he died.

Tiger's Gratitude

A Monument for Brother and Sister

In the Kyeryong Mountains in Ch'ungch'ŏng Province there is a pagoda near a cave located not far away from Tonghak Temple. Long ago a Buddhist monk stayed in this cave disciplining himself in Buddha's teaching. He was a pleasant, big-hearted man, so people thought of "ho," the Chinese character for good, whenever they saw him. But he was more benevolent than anyone else, so they called him Hoho. Monk Hoho.

One night when he was just about to go to bed he heard the cries of a tiger in pain. He went out of the cave to see what was going on and saw a huge white tiger howling, its mouth wide open. Now the monk was a man of strong discipline, and he did not even blink an eye at the sight of the howling tiger. He just approached the tiger to see what was troubling it.

The tiger stopped crying and looked at the monk with pleading eyes. But it kept its mouth wide open. The monk got closer and looked inside its mouth, and discovered a big bone stuck where the jaws join. So the monk reached in and pulled the bone out. Then he gave the tiger a scolding. "You're a tiger, king of the mountains, and you should behave like a king. Choose your food more carefully. Eat wisely, not foolishly like this.

From now on, keep your eyes wide open, and watch what you eat."

About a month later the monk was getting ready for bed when he heard the tiger again. He went outside and saw the tiger with a beautiful young woman in its mouth. The tiger put the unconscious woman down in front of the monk and was gone before the monk had time to ask any questions.

The monk understood why the tiger had brought the lady to him, but, being a monk, he could not take advantage of this beautiful gift in the way the tiger obviously meant him to. For a while he was quite at a loss what to do, but then he realized that he first needed to bring the woman to her senses. He sprinkled some cold water on her face, and she soon came to.

The monk told her what happened, and then asked her how she had got caught by the tiger.

"I am from Ch'angnyŏng, down in Kyŏngsang Province. How that tiger was able to carry me over a hundred miles like this, and so fast, I will never... Anyway, my father is mayor of Ch'angnyŏng, and I'm his only daughter. I love to study the classics, and I even write a poem now and then. Well, last night the moon was bright, and the air was balmy, so I decided to enjoy the moonlight out in the yard and maybe get it to help me with some verses. All I can remember now is seeing that tiger, and then I guess I fainted."

The monk decided to take the young woman back home. They started the long journey to Ch'angnyŏng without delay. After weeks of walking they finally arrived at the woman's home. The mayor thought he was dreaming. His dead daughter had come back to life.

There was a great hullabaloo when the news got out, and the whole city turned out to welcome the woman back.

After hearing his daughter and the monk tell their story, the mayor decided they would naturally have to be formally married, since his daughter had already been with the monk for a long time. The monk tried to convince the man that a Buddhist monk sworn to celibacy would not do what the mayor thought he had done. But the mayor still insisted that the monk take his daughter for his wife.

So the monk had to return to his cave with his new bride. Because of his vows, though, he could not consecrate the marriage. The two discussed the problem, and decided they would become brother and sister. The young woman shaved her head and became a novice. Soon she went to a hermitage deep in the mountains, wearing a cowl on her shaved head.

They devoted themselves to the Buddha and both lived a long life of eighty years. They died at the same time, and after their death the people in that area, who had admired these two over so many years, erected a pagoda in front of the monk's cave in their blessed memory.

The Legend of Hogye Hamlet

In a small hamlet in Anyang County in Kyŏnggi Province, an old woman lived alone with her twelve-year-old son Yŏng-su.

Yŏng-su's father had died when the child was three, and mother and son were left with very little to live on. Yŏng-su took on odd jobs here and there to support his mother, and was known through the hamlet as a dutiful son, but he was really too young to be able to take care of her properly.

Then one day his mother took sick. This was bound to happen, since she never had enough to eat and the house was cold and damp in the winter. The child did not know what to do. He did know, though, that there was no hope. Both of them knew. But he tried to console her and told her she would soon get better.

"My dear boy, I don't think I'll be around much longer," she said one day after about five months of her sickness.

"Mother, don't talk like that. You're not that sick," he answered, very worried.

It was a cold and windy day. It had snowed the whole night through and the snow was knee deep. But Yŏng-su decided he would have to try once more at the medicine shop in the village far away, and he set out into the blistering cold over a path he could not even see under all that snow. But the shop owner would give Yŏng-su nothing because he had no money, and so the boy left the town with great bitterness.

On the way back he grew weary and plopped down in the snow, eyes glazed over with despair. As he huddled in the snow he began to feel cozy and soon began to forget his fatigue and even his worries about his mother. He grew drowsy, and was on the point of dropping off to sleep when an old man with long white hair and beard and a cane in one hand appeared before him. The old man put his hand on Yŏng-su's head and said, "Bless you, my boy. Now up with you, and be on your way."

The boy jumped up in surprise. A mountain spirit? Maybe some medicine! And just then the old man turned into a tiger. Yŏng-su moved back in terror, but the tiger did not do anything besides stand there with his tongue hanging out, panting heavily. Now Yŏng-su could see the tiger was not about to harm him; in fact, the tiger wanted something from him. Water, of course! So Yŏng-su scooped up an armful of snow.

Under the snow, though, he saw a creek. He found a rock and broke the ice, and there was clean, fresh water for the tiger to drink his fill.

After the tiger was satisfied, it gave Yŏng-su a look of gratitude and gestured to the boy to get on its back. Yŏng-su got up on the tiger, and the tiger took him to a cave. Yŏng-su was nervous, but he knew the tiger was not going to hurt him. The tiger walked around the cave for a while, seeming to look for something. Then it stopped and hit the floor of the cave several times with its front paw. It looked at Yŏng-su and wagged its tail.

84 *Tiger, Burning Bright*

Yŏng-su understood and dug a hole at the spot the tiger showed him. There he found a huge aromatic root, which he pulled out and brushed off.

The tiger took Yŏng-su back home on his back. Yŏng-su boiled the root, and after a long time the brew smelled just right. He had his mother drink it down, and right away she was back on her feet.

Today the creek is known as Tiger Creek, and the village is called Hogye-ri, Tiger Creek Hamlet.

Tiger and the Snakes

A country gentry's son with bow and arrows was hurrying on horseback to a neighboring village.

Deep in the forest, far away from any people, he saw a tiger with a snake twined around its waist. He felt sorry for the tiger and, without a second thought, dismounted, climbed a nearby tree and took aim at the snake's darting tongue. He shot an arrow, which hit the snake in the head, and the snake fell to the ground like a lifeless piece of rope.

The man hurried on his way without giving the tiger a second thought. Suddenly, though, he felt something strange in the air and heard a loud hiss. He looked around and saw a huge brown snake bounding toward him. It was the infuriated mate of the snake he had just killed. He spurred his horse to run as fast as it could, but his horse was no match for the snake.

So the man jumped from his horse onto a tree beside the trail. He scrambled up the tree, then turned to find out where the snake was. The snake was certainly able to climb the tree, but for some reason there it was at the bottom, coiled around the tree trunk. It was trying to topple the tree.

The man could not jump down from the tree, so he

just held on with all his might. Then, all of a sudden, the tiger was upon them with a ferocious roar. It started to kick dirt at the snake's head. The snake was so angry that it uncoiled itself from the tree and took off after the tiger.

The tiger ran up to the top of a ridge, turned at a huge boulder, and rolled the boulder back down toward the snake. The boulder rolled right over the snake and squashed the life out of it.

The man continued on his way, completed his business, and returned home safely. He did not know it then, but he was not finished with the tiger yet. One day the tiger gave him a small dog as a gift. The man could not figure out what good a small dog would do him, but he kept and raised it out of gratitude, knowing it's the thought that counts. In the following years, the dog had many puppies.

Three years after he got the dog from the tiger he was coming back from the village study hall. His dogs started barking all at once. The man saw this as an omen and packed his family to move to a different house that very day. When they asked him what this was all about he told them the experience he had had with the tiger and the snake three years before.

He told his family not to tell anyone, not even their closest neighbors, where they were moving. Months passed in their new house peacefully, and then one day the man visited the old house. A cold shudder ran through him when he saw it was full of snakes.

He realized that they had taken over the house to revenge the death of their parents.

So now at last he knew why his tiger friend had given him that small dog.

The Woodcutter and Tiger Cub

There was once a widower whose name was Pak. He lived all alone on the ridge of a high mountain. He was not a man of learning, but he was known as a man of sterling character and was well respected.

His forefathers had been woodcutters, and he was one himself. Every day he gathered wood on the mountain to exchange for food. However, he could not always depend on the mountain for his livelihood, so he planted bamboo around his house and sold this too.

He took great pleasure in watching the bamboo shoots grow, and every morning he checked them before leaving for the mountains to gather firewood.

One year the sprouts were all up in a nice fresh green and he felt very good to think that they would bring in a small fortune for him. But one morning, to his dismay, he found that all the young green sprouts had disappeared. Near his bamboo patch he spotted the tracks of some animal and decided to follow them. He soon came to a bamboo thicket so dense he could not get through, and here he also lost sight of the tracks he was following. So he returned home.

The next day he was back at the bamboo thicket, this time with a spear. Muttering and sputtering to himself

90 Tiger, Burning Bright

what a lesson he would certainly teach to the insolent beast who had stolen his bamboo sprouts, he pushed his way through the high, closely packed bamboo.

After a long struggle he came upon a tiger cub. The cub was too young to know that he was supposed to be afraid of this animal with two legs, and it did nothing to get away. The man, knowing the cub was the cause of his disaster, was tempted to kill the cub right on the spot, but when he looked into its innocent eyes he dropped his spear. He left his spear there and returned home, and never mentioned the affair to anyone.

After the woodcutter left, the cub's mother returned to the bamboo thicket with food. She saw the man's spear and the horrible realization dawned on her that her cub could have been killed. Putting two and two together the tigress figured out what had happened.

Being an intelligent animal the tigress decided to repay the woodcutter for his kindness. She hunted down a wild boar and left it in the man's yard. And she continued to do this with different game every so often throughout the rest of her life. All this time and ever thereafter no villagers were ever harmed again by a tiger.

Tiger for a Son

Back near the turn of the century in Ch'ŏngp'yŏng township, Kyŏnggi Province, about ten miles south of where the big dam is now, there was a hamlet of only six households called Serak. The hamlet's families lived happily, like one big family.

But there was an old couple living among them, two poor but good and upright people, who were not so happy. They had no children and lived a rather lonely life.

They had not always been childless. They had once had a healthy and handsome son who was more precious to them than gold or jade. But when he was twelve he was killed by a tiger on his way home from an errand to a neighboring village about fifteen *ri* away.

It was a stunning tragedy for the couple. They wanted to see him grow up and raise his own family and were counting on him to care for them in their old age. After this sudden loss of all their hopes, they aged quickly. Life lost all of its joy for them.

It was no use to try to console them. And their insides burned with a desire to avenge their son's death. So they always carried a weapon whenever they went to chop wood or pick ferns in the mountains, ready for the time they would have the luck to come upon a tiger. Any tiger.

Meanwhile, the old lady's despair grew so great that it made her ill. In that small mountain hamlet there was no medicine, and though there was some in the neighboring village, the old couple could not afford it. And so the woman died.

The old man was now lonelier than ever. He spent most of his time in the mountains, apparently with the idea that the less he saw of people the less he would be reminded of his son and wife.

One day, at dusk, he went deeper into the mountains than he ever had before. Looking at the beautiful sky created by the setting sun he started thinking again about his son and wife.

Suddenly, a strange noise brought him back. He looked around, and there he saw a little tiger trying desperately to get out of a deep pool of water. The old man pulled the cub out of the water. It was out of breath and nearly dead, so he rushed home with the cub. From then on he took care of the growing tiger as if it were his own son. He began to feel better, and looked happy and full of life.

The tiger had a strong affection for the old man, too. It grew bigger and stronger and helped its companion with chores at home. And they were happy together.

But then one day the old man became sick. Three days later he died. The tiger mourned for three days, like a good son, and then took the old man to the mountain and gave him a proper burial.

And after that no one ever saw the tiger again.

Tiger the Matchmaker

The Matchmaking Mountain Spirit

K_{im}, a man of the gentry, had a daughter whose name was Ok-bun. Her beauty was often compared to the rising moon.

Pak, a commoner, lived in the same village, and had a son whose name was P'al-bong. He was often compared to the rising sun.

The two young ones were of different social class, but they were very close, as they had been playing together ever since they were little children. They especially liked going hiking together in the mountains, Ok-bun with her herb basket and P'al-bong with his A-frame.

As they got older Ok-bun's father could see that they were getting serious about each other, and he did not want his daughter to get any mischievous ideas about marrying some commoner. What a waste of a good name that would be. He was determined to marry his daughter to Tol-swae, also the son of gentry. So he told his daughter to stop meeting P'al-bong, scolding harshly that it was improper for a young lady of her class to be tramping around with a no-account of his sort.

Ok-bun did not have the heart to disobey her father, and at the same time she despaired over her impending separation from P'al-bong. She lost her appetite, then lost weight, and then became absolutely emaciated. Her father did not worry too much, though. He knew she would forget P'al-bong once she married and settled down. But her marriage would have to happen before she wasted away to absolutely nothing, so he quickly arranged for the engagement and set an early wedding date.

P'al-bong felt wretched. Whenever the thought of losing Ok-bun hit him, just because of the class system, he gritted his teeth and his eyes became fiery balls of pure fury. But neither P'al-bong nor his father had the power to do anything to prevent Ok-bun's marriage and bring her back to him.

Ok-bun's wedding day soon came. After a splendid feast the bridegroom entered the bridal chamber, where Ok-bun was waiting for him. Following tradition, he took off her headgear and removed her outer clothing, piece by fragrant piece. Then he put out the light, all set to climb in bed with her.

And then... What's that! A tiger in our own bedroom! There was such a ruckus that everybody in the house was soon scrambling in all directions. In all the turmoil the tiger escaped with the new bride.

Our grief-stricken P'al-bong and his father, of course, had not attended the wedding. They were now at home, fast asleep. But then they were wakened by a loud thump in the next room. When they went there to see what was going on, they were shocked to discover none other than Ok-bun lying there unconscious on the floor.

In the meantime Tol-swae had got together a search party to find the tiger and its victim. They were hunting all over the area for them, while others stayed at home and tried to console her father.

P'al-bong's father, a righteous man, felt obliged to report what had happened, so he went to Ok-bun's father and explained everything in detail. On hearing this everyone nodded and said that it was the mountain spirit at its matchmaking again, and that no human should interfere. What else could Ok-bun's father do but go along with this? Even her bridegroom saw that their marriage could not be. And so a marriage between Ok-bun and P'al-bong was arranged.

And the childhood sweethearts lived happily ever after.

The Woodcutter and the Bandit's Foster Daughter

Ilsan Peak, mountain of two rivers, rises three hundred meters above sea level. It sits to the south of Muhan Creek and to the north of the clear blue Kŭm River. There was nothing special about this mountain to draw anyone's attention—just some round, bare peaks in front of one higher round, bare peak, not all that uncommon a sight in Korea. On one ridge of this mountain, though, was a huge rock thirty meters high, and under this rock was a cave, into which no one had ever dared venture. It was a tiger cave.

At the foot of Ilsan Peak nestled a village. Its name was Ch'ŏngsu-ri, because it was blessed with a crystal clear stream that never dried up. In this village there lived a thirty-year-old bachelor who they called "Old bachelor Chŏng-dol" because he was several years past the usual marrying age. This Chŏng-dol still wore the pig-tail that unmarried young people had to wear in those days. A diligent man, he gathered wood around Ilsan Peak every day, rain or shine, and sold it at Ch'ŏngyang, a town about twenty *ri* away. He was said to have saved up quite a lot of money, what with his diligence and almost no one to spend his money on. But he did have his widowed old mother, and this good-natured man was very devoted to her.

Chŏng-dol thought that he should not marry, so that he could devote all his attention to his mother. His mother, on the other hand, wished with all her heart that he would marry, so that at least she could hold her grandchild in her arms before she died.

One day, when Chŏng-dol was chopping wood in the mountains, he came upon several tiger cubs playing in the sun near a huge old tree. Fascinated by the cute little tigers, and never giving a thought to when their mother would return, he fondled them and fed them fried bean patties which he had brought for lunch.

The tiger cubs evoked feelings of love that he had never experienced. He fell in love with the cubs as he stroked them and watched them play. He was so engrossed in them that he completely forgot about the wood that he should be chopping. But then, when the sun began to sink, he remembered his mother and hurried down the mountain with his half-empty A-frame on his back.

By and by, three years passed. Chŏng-dol was still a bachelor, and his mother still dreamed of holding that grandchild in her arms. One day as the sun was setting he was on his way home with a load of leaves, sticks and twigs. As he carefully threaded his way down the path with his heavy load something sped past him. When he was finally able to make out what it was, his eyes popped in surprise. A tiger holding a woman in its mouth!

Without a thought for his own safety he jumped into action. He threw his A-frame off his back and took after the tiger. He chased the beast over hill and dale, shout-

The Woodcutter and the Bandit's Foster Daughter

ing at it to stop.

Then, all of a sudden it did stop. The man also stopped. Then the tiger turned on him. The man tried to figure out what to do now that he had got his wish. He took a step backward. The tiger took a step forward. The man took another step back, and the tiger took another ahead. They went on like this, a step for a step, for a while, until the beast finally got tired of it and just dropped the woman's body on the ground. He roared one last roar, turned, and vanished.

When the man was finally able to gather his wits about him he approached the woman, who was lying very still. She was unconscious, but she was alive. She was also young and beautiful. The man carried her down the mountain to his house.

The woman regained consciousness and told Chŏng-dol and his mother that she had lived deep in the mountains until seven years before, when she was fourteen. Then she was taken off by bandits to a mountain fortress and made to serve their chief. Contrary to what you would expect, the chief did not make a concubine of her. Instead he treated her like his own daughter. And so she had been with those bandits until the tiger caught her at the well.

The bachelor's mother, of course, was exceedingly happy to hear this story. She ran all over the village telling everyone that the mountain spirit had arranged a wife for her son. This was a marriage made in heaven.

And, sure enough, the woodcutter and the bandits' woman lived happily together for the rest of their lives.

Charcoal Burner and Lady Scholar

During the reign of King Sukjong, toward the end of the seventeenth century, there lived in a remote mountain village of Ch'ungch'ŏng Province a man named Kim Sam-gil. He was almost thirty, but still single, and supported his parents. His mother was aged, and his father was aged and sick. Deep in the mountains as he was, all he could do to supplement his family's meager living was work his own small vegetable patch and peddle charcoal. He had to walk fifty *ri* to the market at Myŏnch'ŏn to sell his charcoal.

From childhood he was strong as a horse but agile as a swallow. The strong are often said to be slow of wit; but Sam-gil was as quick and intelligent as he was strong.

One cool, breezy day in late fall, when the valley floor was thickly covered with fallen leaves, Sam-gil had just finished chopping wood and started picking wild grapes. This may sound like work, but he enjoyed this immensely. He became so absorbed in his work that he went deeper and deeper into the woods, farther than he had ever been before, farther than human footsteps had ever trod, where straight pines, crooked pines, oaks, and all sorts of vegetation grew twice as big and three times as thick as they do where humans tread.

It was already well past lunch time and nearing the time for his late afternoon snack. But Sam-gil thought he had better get back to chopping some more wood before he rested. He set down his A-frame and was just raising his ax when he heard a woman's giggle. He could not believe his ears. He waited, and heard it again. This time it was a full, rolling laugh that seemed it could not control itself. But it was without a doubt the laughter of a woman.

"Strange," thought Sam-gil. "So deep in the forest." Then he got the notion that maybe some fox had turned itself into a woman to cast a spell on him. He strained his ears to listen again.

And there it was again. He could not ignore the laughter or pretend he had not heard it, though he knew he should. He began to walk carefully toward the sound.

Then he stopped short. His eyes widened as they focused upon a scene they could not believe. On a round rock down in the valley a white tiger as big as a house was tickling a young woman.

In those days it was said that a tiger would grab a human, take the person deep into the mountains, and play a while with its victim before finally devouring its meal. The victim would usually die laughing.

Sam-gil flew as fast as the wind and jumped on the tiger from behind. He got his hands around its throat and squeezed with all his might. Even this tiger as huge as a mountain could not overcome Sam-gil's strength. The tiger kicked and punched with an insane fury, but then it stopped, and soon went limp. Sam-gil knew the tiger was dead but he wanted to make sure, so he broke its enormous head against a rock.

The exhausted woman lost consciousness in her sudden relief. Sam-gil scooped some spring water in his hands and moistened her lips. Then he put the young woman on his back and returned home. He lay her down on the heated floor, washed her with warm water, and spoon-fed her a bowl of gruel.

Finally, after a while she had regained enough strength to start wondering what was happening. "What am I doing here? How did I get here?"

"We'll talk about it later. Pull yourself together first."

Sam-gil's parents were very happy that their son had saved a girl from a tiger. "Now you two are getting married. It's heaven's will as plain as can be."

"I can't expect her to be my wife just because I rescued her. I'm taking her home."

Sam-gil was thinking that what had happened was no more than that one human had saved another human. If she had no idea of marrying him, it would not be fair of him to push her. Sam-gil, with his big heart, was happy enough that he had been able to help her. He would never think for a moment of taking advantage of the young woman.

A couple of days went by and the young woman recovered from the shock of her encounter with the tiger. She was finally able to tell Sam-gil the whole story. She was the only daughter of a Hong in Yŏngdong, Ch'ungch'ŏng Province. She remembered going outside to the toilet and then, on her way back into her house, being carried away by the tiger; but what happened after that she remembered very little. The young woman concluded it must have been heaven's will that she was saved at that critical moment. And she ended her story by telling Sam-gil she couldn't thank him enough.

Sam-gil said, "I guess you ought to go back home now that you've recovered. Your family must be worried sick over you."

This made the maiden feel even more grateful to Sam-gil. She saw he must be nearly thirty, and still not married. He had saved her life; he was strong enough to kill that tiger with his bare hands. Illiterate he was, but his deportment was noble, and she saw now that men did good deeds because of a noble personality, not because of knowledge. And she made up her mind to marry this man.

The young woman looked full into Sam-gil's face. "I would be dead now if it hadn't been for your great kindness. And since you have seen my body unclothed, I cannot marry any other man. I wish you would let me repay your kindness by serving you as your wife."

"It's kind of you to say that, lovely maiden. You'd have to get your parents' permission first, though, before you make up your mind. But it would certainly be a great honor to have you as my wife."

With this the young woman admired him all the more.

So Sam-gil took her home to Yŏngdong. Her father had given up all hope of ever seeing her alive again. He could not believe his eyes when he saw a young man approaching with his daughter.

Her father listened to the amazing report of how Sam-gil had saved his daughter's life. He not only felt grateful to Sam-gil for having saved his daughter but was also very impressed with the way he had made her get her parents' permission to marry. Such an extremely dependable and admirable young man! And he readily agreed to this marriage.

Sam-gil and his wife returned to Myŏnch'ŏn and earned their livelihood selling charcoal. Then one day his wife suggested, "You know, you were never meant to sell charcoal all your life. Why don't you study, and try for a position in the government?"

"How can I study with us as far away from any school as we are?"

"That's no problem. I know how to read. Would you mind learning from me?"

Her father, having no sons, had taught his only daughter the Confucian classics, and she had turned out to be an excellent student. So Sam-gil and his wife studied together every evening after they were finished with their work. They started with the basic Thousand Characters text, and his wife found him intelligent and quick to learn. In five years he learned all his wife could teach him.

With this much learning under his belt, Sam-gil quit his charcoal selling and went up to Seoul. He became a pupil of Song Si-yŏl, the renowned scholar known also as U-am, who taught him more of the classics and rites and introduced him to other great scholars. Sam-gil, with his quick and deep intelligence, was Master Song's favorite. The Master expected big things from him.

Sam-gil's wife was very happy that her husband had become a scholar. Though housekeeping on her meager income was a painful chore, she kept their home with a cheerful heart. To keep her new parents reasonably comfortable she worked hard washing and sewing for other families and doing other odd jobs. It was a happy household, made so by this good woman.

When Sam-gil was in his forties he took the higher civil service examination and, to no one's surprise, scored highest. He was admitted into the Academy of Letters, whose members in addition to their official duties discussed literature in the presence of the King at every royal banquet. This was quite a prestigious position for the former charcoal seller. He also won the King's favor, and was appointed Minister of Finance, in charge of the nation's treasury. As you would expect, though, other ministers endlessly petitioned the King in protest against Sam-gil's appointment on the grounds of his low birth. The King responded to their petitions by promoting Sam-gil one step higher for each petition against his appointment. The King was determined to enforce his policy of appointing good men to high positions, whatever their origin, so that the country could be served faithfully. Sam-gil was both very grateful and deeply impressed by the ways of the King, and he was determined to devote his life to this King and his nation.

King Sukjong was deeply concerned about the welfare of his people. He often sneaked out of his palace in commoner's attire to make the rounds of the capital. He appointed Sam-gil Inspector of the Three Southern Provinces and ordered him to go and see how people were faring there. Sam-gil accomplished his task in a way that surprised even this King who had such high expectations of him, and the King appointed him Minister of Culture and Education.

To this day we can see a stone monument in Chŏng-san, Ch'ungch'ŏng Province, praising Kim Sam-gil's virtue and achievements.

Tiger and Famous
Historical Personages

General Kang and the Tigers

During the reign of King Hyŏnjong, in the eleventh-century of the Koryŏ dynasty, a detached palace was built in the new city of Hanyang, which we know today as Seoul. The King's palace was in Kaesŏng, in the north, but he occasionally stayed in Hanyang so that he could give attention to his people in the southern half of the country.

At that time Seoul was a small town, a place of mountains, trees and wild animals. In the mountains surrounding the city—Pugak and Samgak to its back in the north, Inwang in the west, and Namsan to the south with Kwanak even further south, across the river—the trees grew so dense that it was all but impossible to see the sky through them. One can imagine how difficult it was to get around the area at night.

The people in this village had begun to worry about all the tigers and wolves that preyed not only on small animals but also, recently, on humans. After the sun set people could not even visit a neighbor without fear of being eaten up by one of these beasts.

At that time the area around what today we call Chongno 4-ga was called One Hundred Hill. It got its name when it was discovered that tigers would not attack when a crowd of about a hundred crossed it making a racket with their gongs and drums.

So the villagers held a meeting to discuss ways to rid themselves of the tigers. "Isn't this nonsense when we, the lords of creation, cannot go out of our houses and are so helpless after the sun sets? We cannot hunt down and kill every tiger, of course, but neither can we stay inside and worry all the time. We must come up with a way to get rid of these blasted creatures."

"Listen! How about asking that great general Kang Kam-ch'an to help us out? You heard how he solved the problem of all those noisy frogs in Haeju, how he struck them all dumb."

"Good idea! If someone like him came here the tigers would be too scared to even think about harming people. But as the old saying goes, 'Strike while the iron is hot,' so let's quit talking and appoint several of us right now to leave for the capital. We'll take a petition to General Kang telling him how we just can't go on living like this and ask him to come and stay here with us a while." So they wrote the petition and left for Kaesŏng even before the ink was dry.

A few days later Kang Kam-ch'an was entering the royal palace in his palanquin, when he accidentally came upon a red gate ghost following a wedding party. When the ghost realized who was following it fled in terror before General Kang could even lift a finger to scare him away. Inside the palace he told the King his funny story.

The King replied with a smile and a request. "General Kang, you must do us a favor again, indisposed as you may be in your old age."

Looking up at the King, General Kang answered,

"Your majesty, whatever you may ask, how would I dare but to obey? I'll go through fire and water to comply with your majesty's august command." And he put the final touch on his flamboyant expression of loyalty with a deep bow.

The King took another look at the petition he had received just the day before. He spoke slowly, "Listen, General. We have here a petition from the people of Hanyang. They say they can hardly live there anymore because the tigers there frequently prey on them. I had thought of just sending a band of hunters to get rid of the evil creatures. But in their petition they ask specifically for you to come and stay there a while. It seems that even the people of Hanyang have heard of your valor. They seem to expect you to strike all the tigers there dumb and prevent them from injuring any more people, like you did when you took care of your ten thousand frogs. How about it, General, won't you go there for a while and give them some relief?"

Moved by the King's gentle request, General Kang bowed deep again and said, "It is certainly gracious of you to tell me that people speak so highly of an old man like me. I'm flattered they have such high regard for me. So what else can I do but comply with your order? Even if it meant my death, it would be honorable if it were in your service. I'll leave at once."

The King nodded approvingly. He appointed General Kang supervisor of the royal palace in Hanyang and threw a great feast, attended by all his court, to bid the general farewell.

General Kang departed for his new post the next day. The people of Hanyang got the good news and came out as far as Koyang to welcome him. Walking slowly in the midst of this great throng, trying to calm their fears, General Kang entered the palace.

Strangely enough, not a single tiger appeared after the arrival of General Kang. Everyone said it was natural, that the tigers were in a state of shock. General Kang was the talk of the town.

"Didn't I tell you? You remember I said everything would be all right if only General Kang would come. And see, as soon as he arrives the tigers are stopped in their tracks. I say this man was sent by heaven. It looks as if he's turned every one of those tigers into stone."

"Of course. Just like I said it would turn out. Those frogs at Puyong-dang in Haeju, the way they ruined everyone's sleep and work, they sure found out what's what when General Kang was appointed magistrate of Haeju. You don't hear from those frogs anymore. So what more is there to say? Now we can relax and breathe easy."

"But what'll we do when he leaves and the tigers come back?"

"Coward! Anyway, do you think he'd just leave, without doing something first to take care of things for good? He'll go back when he's good and ready, and that won't be till he's taught our tigers some manners."

Then one day, about a month after the general's arrival, a crowd of people were talking about him when a man rushed up to them, wide-eyed and gasping for breath. He could hardly get a word out, he was so excited. "Listen, everyone! Something horrible's happened!"

"What's the big fuss there?"

Still gasping, the man managed, "You think I'm making this big fuss as you call it just for some fun? The tigers are back, that's the big fuss."

Everyone looked at each other in disbelief. "No, that can't be true! The General's frightened them all off. But come on, tell us more. What... Where... When...?"

"Does this mean General Kang can't help us anymore?"

"Nonsense. But it does seem we have a problem."

Amid all this tongue-clicking and worried looks the man who brought the news said in a trembling voice, "We're in big trouble. In a village just a few *ri* off a tiger came down from the mountain and carried off a child. And in another village not far from there a young man was done in by a tiger on his way back from market. So who knows? Anything could happen to us, any time."

As the rumors spread the fear grew. The representatives of each village got together to discuss what to do. First they decided that every villager should burn a torch and strike the gongs throughout the night, starting at dusk, and that the young men should stand guard all night. In addition, the representatives visited the palace to petition an audience with General Kang.

The old man was surprised. "I thought those tigers must have learned some common sense, since we haven't heard anything from them for all this time now." He pulled at his beard and mumbled to himself, "I wonder why they've started attacking people again. I was going to leave them alone, but now I guess I'll have to do something."

So he wrote a talisman on a yellow piece of paper and called two robust servants. "Take this to the temple halfway up Inwang Mountain. You'll find an old monk there. Give it to him."

The servants took the talisman, but looked at each other with puzzled expressions. "But General, he must be in league with the tigers; otherwise how could he live there? Shouldn't we capture the monk?"

General Kang smiled. "No, there's no need to do that.

Just give him the talisman. And be very polite to him if you want to come back alive."

"Yes, sir. We shall carry out your order without fail," they said and left.

They certainly did not want to go up that mountain, and they definitely did not want to meet that old monk. But they trusted their benevolent master, and believed that he would not send them to their death. So they climbed the mountain and finally saw the monk off in the distance, sitting on a rock in the sun, placidly picking lice from his clothes.

"Well, that must be him. Let's give this to him and then get out of here. If we hang around here we're liable to become a tiger's meal. But I just don't get it. We asked General Kang to do something about the tigers to stop them from attacking us, and what does he do but order us to give a talisman to a monk who's probably bosom buddies with those same tigers."

"Stop complaining," said his friend. "Anyway, let's be very careful, and very nice. The General must have some reason for telling us to treat the monk with kid gloves."

Soon they arrived in front of the monk. One of them said, "Please take this. It is from General Kang Kam-ch'an." The old monk looked at them furtively, and nodded. They quickly left as soon as he began reading the message.

Just as they returned to the palace to report on their mission someone rushed in with a message for the general, so the servants were kept waiting. But they peeped into the hall through the cracks in the door and were shocked to see the monk they had just left at Inwang Mountain being ushered into the General's presence.

"What! How could such an old man get here so fast?

And you know how fast we ran back here. The guy must be superhuman."

They kept on peeking through the door, and now saw the old monk get down to his knees in front of the dais where the General sat.

General Kang cleared his throat, then boomed in a thundering voice which seemed to shake the rafters, "Listen here, you scoundrel. You can take off that disguise right now."

Immediately the old monk turned a couple somersaults in the air, and what landed was no monk but a tiger. He sat on his haunches and hung his head.

The eavesdropping servants were so frightened they could hardly catch a breath. They watched frozen in shock.

The General scolded the tiger. "You may be beneath humans, but you are still king of beasts. So I thought you would be different from other animals, maybe have some more intelligence. But you don't act all that smart. How dare you gobble up humans, the lords of creation, as if they were some midnight snack! How could you be so dumb you don't know there is divine punishment in store for those who commit such dastardly deeds? On behalf of heaven I should stop wasting my time and just destroy the whole lot of you. The whole lot, and you first! But, as heaven is merciful, I won't. Not this time anyway. If you and your mob don't clear out of Korea, and if you even think of disobeying me, just one more time, I'll not only kill you but also banish your species forever from the earth. Now what have you got to say about that?"

The tiger hung its head, weeping silently. Then all of a sudden the General caught himself. "Oh, how thoughtless can I get! You can't talk in your present form. Go on, change back to human. At once."

The tiger turned a couple somersaults in the air and landed back on his feet as the old monk. He bowed politely to the General and, wiping away his tears with the back of his hand, said, "There are several really diabolical ones among us. They're the ones causing all the trouble. And I've been trying to come up all this time with a way to stop them. Now though, by your gracious favor, heaven is holding back its vengeance. I shall never forget your kindness as long as I live. But General, where can we go so all of a sudden, being so many of us? We'll go, yes. But please, tell us where."

The General thought for a long time, and then said in a solemn voice, "All right, now listen close. If you cross the border at the Yalu River and continue on across the Yodong Plain about seven hundred *ri*, you will find Kollyun Mountain. A dense forest a thousand years old covers that mountain. I think it would be a good place for you to live. It's a nice place, a big place with an inexhaustible supply of food for you and all the others, so you won't have any excuse to go eating humans again. If you do attack anyone in those villages around the mountain, if you touch one hair on one beggar's head, that's it. I'll send the punishment of heaven down on your heads so fast and so hard you'll never know what hit you."

The old monk bowed deeply several times. "As you say, General. When do you want us to leave?"

General Kang thought a while about this one too. Then he counted to himself on the fingers of his left hand, finally nodded to himself and told the old monk, "Today is the last day of the fourth moon. Cross the Yalu at midnight of the fifteenth day of the fifth moon, when everyone is sleeping. I do feel somewhat sorry you all have to move like this, so I'll see you off at the Yalu that day, maybe have some food fixed up for you. Now, go and prepare for your journey."

The old monk bowed several times to the General, then came out through the door the servants were peeping through. The servants scrambled to hide, then watched. As the monk walked down the long corridor he vanished. The servants finally managed to stop gawking and rushed to their homes, where they boasted about all they had witnessed.

The news spread quickly. Naturally, everyone in Hanyang came to know about it, and started feeling very good that from that day on they would be able to live without any anxiety about where the tigers' next meal would come from.

Kang Kam-ch'an ordered his servants to prepare for his journey to the Yalu. They cooked dozens of dogs and pigs and loaded them on horses. The General arrived at the river on the fourteenth day of the fifth moon, the day before the tigers were supposed to cross. The next evening, right on schedule, several thousand tigers showed up. General Kang gave the pigs and dogs to the monk, who brought the tigers as he had promised.

"I am sending you tigers away, but I am sorry to make you go like this. I wish there could have been some other way. Anyway, here's the food I said I would prepare for you. Eat it all now, because you'll need every bit of energy you can get to cross that river."

The old monk was so profoundly moved by the General's generosity that he bowed deeply several times. "We thank heaven for the warm heart it gave you, General. You needn't have gone through all this trouble for us. But look at me! I'm ashamed, because I

General Kang and the Tigers   121

have just one last favor to ask."

"What is it then?"

"You see, there is a pregnant tiger among us. She hasn't the strength to cross that river. She even has trouble walking now, and breathes with great difficulty. Will you please let her stay?"

"All right. Pregnancy is just as difficult for beasts as it is for humans. I really have no choice, I guess. But she must leave after her cubs are born."

And the word has been passed down from generation to generation that the few tigers living in Korea today are the offspring of that one pregnant tiger that stayed.

The Tiger and Sŏ Hwadam

Yŏnsan-gun, the fifteenth-century king of Korea, carried out an unrelenting persecution of Confucian scholars who were opposed to his reign. Because of this most scholars lived a life of isolation in the mountains or in remote corners of the provinces, abandoning the chaotic world of politics and power struggles. As they immersed themselves in learning, Confucian thought advanced at a striking pace.

After Yŏnsan-gun lost the throne, Chungjong was king. The persecution stopped, but many Confucian scholars preferred to continue their retirement in the remote provinces. At this time there lived a man named Sŏ Kyŏng-dŏk, whose honorary name was Hwadam. He never held a government position, but was well known throughout the country as a great scholar and teacher.

One day he was holding class with the door of the schoolhouse wide open. He was teaching his students the Chinese classics when he noticed an old monk passing by out in front of the school. This monk was wearing gentry clothing and carrying a sack. The teacher stopped and watched the passing monk, then told one of his students to call the monk back.

"Where are you going?" he demanded. "Tell me the truth, now."

The monk, as if sensing something from the unusual tone of the teacher's question, cringed and answered humbly, "Your humble servant is going to a feast."

"And at what time is this feast supposed to begin?"

"At seven this evening. Pray forgive me and let me pass." The monk bowed his head and walked quickly away.

"That monk is actually a tiger," the teacher told his students. "I think he is going to try to carry off the bride at a wedding feast."

"She must be warned!" cried the students.

"Yes, someone must go and warn them. Now, which of you knows the preface to the Doctrine of the Mean? That's the only thing that can protect her."

Immediately one student volunteered to go.

"Go to the wedding feast then, and persuade the family not to leave the bride alone in the nuptial chamber but to sit close together around her. At midnight, you must sit just inside the door and recite the preface incessantly, until the cock crows at dawn. This has been used since ancient times as an incantation for repelling ghosts. Then come back here."

The student left at once for the wedding feast. When he arrived the feast had already begun and the house was bustling with activity. He persuaded the family to do as his teacher had instructed. When midnight came on he began reciting the preface. The family, frightened as they were, all sat there without a word.

Then suddenly a violent wind blew up and a tiger appeared in the house with a thundering roar. It kicked hard at the door to the nuptial chamber, but the door did not yield. It stepped back and tried again. And again, and again. The family inside was scared out of their minds, and the bride even fainted. While they sat huddled in fear, the student continued to recite the preface.

At long last the cock crowed, and at that instant the

tiger disappeared. Then the student stopped his recitation and had the family massage the bride to bring her to her senses, and bid them feed her thin rice gruel to give her some strength. When the bride looked as if she would recover completely, the student returned to the schoolhouse, where his teacher was waiting for him.

Later that day the teacher saw the same monk crossing the school yard again, from the direction of the wedding feast. He called to the monk and asked, "Why are you coming back empty-handed?"

"Yesterday I tried to escort that bride to Tiger Mountain, where she is destined to go. But I could not enter her room because it was surrounded by a fence. But there was a hole in it, so I was struggling to enter through that hole, and was just about to enter the room, when the cock crowed. That's why I'm coming back empty-handed. Because of you I wasn't able to accomplish my task." The monk bowed politely and walked off briskly.

The teacher called to the student and told him, grinning, "You recited some phrases incorrectly yesterday."

"Oh no, Master! I recited every word carefully, without making a single mistake."

The teacher thought this strange. He knew that the hole in the fence was caused by the student's mistakes. So he asked him to recite the preface again. The student did and the teacher found that he did indeed make several mistakes. When the teacher pointed out these mistakes, the student blushed deeply.

Mistakes or no mistakes, however, the point is that Hwadam saved the bride's life.

The Tiger and Kim Ŭng-sŏ

One clear day a big tiger, disguising himself as a monk, was on his way to Yonggang in P'yŏngan Province. The mountain spirit had told him a tiger can turn himself into a human if he eats a virgin, and he was on his way to find his meal.

He had just arrived at a major thoroughfare when a man approached him and asked for directions to Yonggang. The tiger monk proposed they go together, as he was also going to Yonggang. As they traveled along together the traveller noticed that the monk's behavior was rather strange. But, thinking that everyone has his own idiosyncrasies, he did not mention anything.

That evening, when they had almost reached Yonggang, the monk told his traveling companion his reason for visiting the place. "Although I look like a monk, I am really a tiger. One day I prayed to the mountain spirit to make me a human, and he told me that I could become a human if I ate a virgin from Yonggang. So what is your business in Yonggang?"

And the traveler ran away in a panic.

On arriving at Yonggang the monk went to the place the mountain spirit had told him to go, and saw a woman plowing in a field. He circled her, carefully,

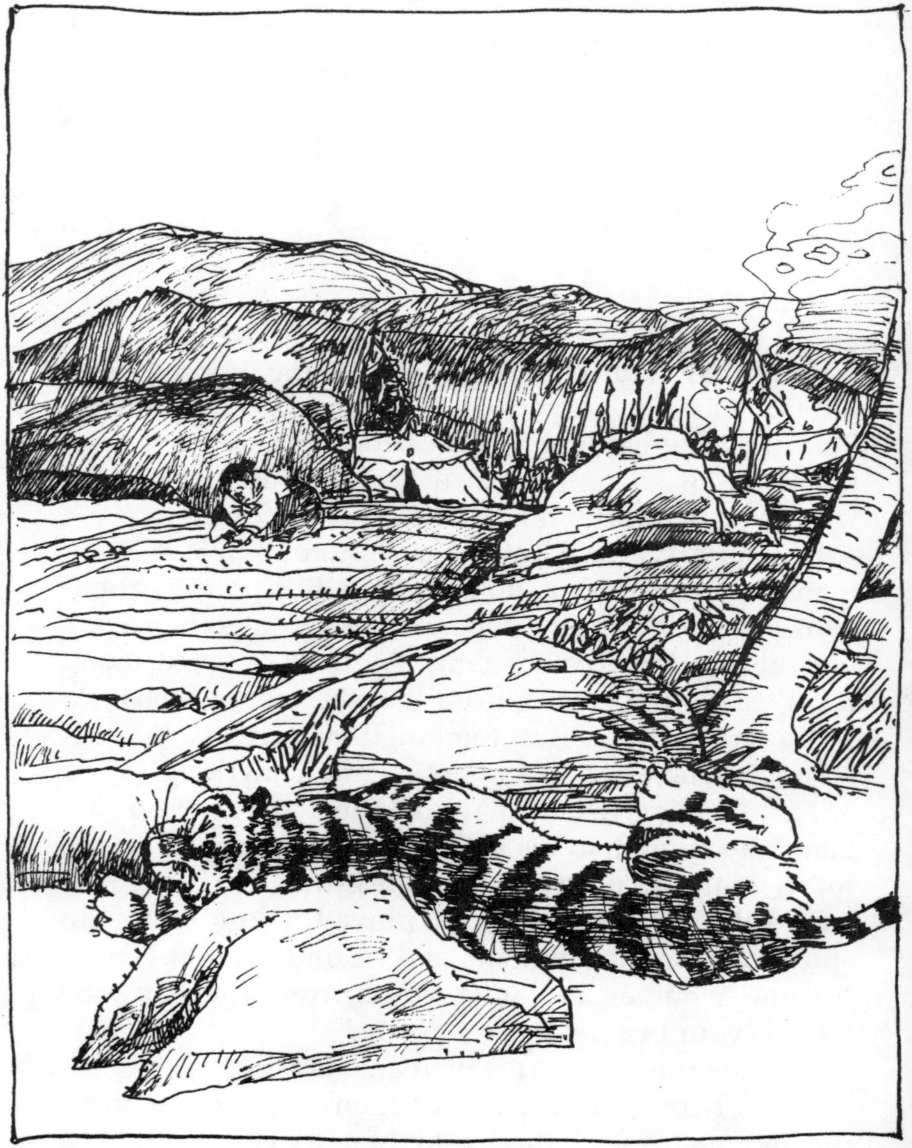

round and round. But after completing several turns, he fell down dead and turned into the corpse of a tiger.

This happened to the hapless tiger because the woman was pregnant with a child destined to serve his country as a great hero, and she and her child were being protected by a large army of spirits. The tiger sensed this and, knowing it could not defeat this army, killed itself. It thought it was better to die as a monk than to continue life as a tiger.

The next day the traveler who met the monk the day before was passing by the field and saw the dead tiger. He carried it off to the market and sold it for a lot of money.

After some time the woman gave birth to a boy. This boy grew up rapidly and became a man of tremendous strength and prowess. His name was Kim Ŭng-sŏ, the great hero of olden times.

The Tiger and Kwak Chae-u

Back in the sixteenth century, in Sangju, Kyŏngsang Province, there lived a man named Kwak Chae-u. Everyone knows the story of how this young man, burning with a sense of justice, raised a volunteer army and repulsed the Japanese when they invaded Korea.

But how did all this come to pass? One day, in the thirty-first year of the reign of King Sŏnjo, a year before the Japanese invasion, Kwak Chae-u went to the woods a little way off from his village to practice in the martial arts. Deep inside this forest of huge trees and giant rocks he practiced with his sword, occasionally encouraging himself by shouting "Yah! Ho!" at the sky with all his strength. After practicing for a while he washed himself with the clear water which flowed from the hollow of a rock, then prayed to the mountain spirit. When he departed for home the sun was beginning to set in the west. Brave he was, but he also knew the danger of being in the woods all by himself. He had a healthy fear and, although he tried to shake off his fear by quickening his steps, his mind was racing ahead of him.

He turned a bend in the path, expecting to see the lights of the village. Instead, he saw the bright, menacing lights of a tiger's eyes. The tiger, as big as a boulder and with eyes the size of saucers, was blocking his way and did not look as if it were about to move. Kwak's hair stood on end, his spine tingled, and his whole body trembled. Nonetheless he pulled himself together and, remembering all that he had practiced earlier that day, rushed to the tiger, aiming to finish it off with a thrust of his sword into the tiger's most vulnerable spot. The next moment he found himself lying next to a rock, his sword stuck in the ground at his side. Strange! He was sure he had got the tiger right where he wanted to.

He looked around for the tiger. It was backing away quickly. Kwak attacked again, but the tiger finessed again, then stopped a short distance away. Kwak attacked again and again, but each time the tiger sidestepped him and stood there a few feet further away, just watching.

Before long the moon was high up in the sky. And still Kwak continued his attack. Man and tiger ran through thorn bush and thicket, across rice paddy and plain. Finally, after crossing six streams and three mountains, they found themselves in a deep forest of pine trees. Kwak followed the tiger along a meandering path to a cave with a big boulder for a door. The tiger ran into the cave, but when Kwak tried to follow it in, he could not get through the tightly closed stone door. Then how did the tiger get in? He put his ear to the door but could not hear a sound inside.

Kwak thought it extremely odd that this long chase had ended in such a bizarre way. But, since he could not break down the door, he gave up with a shrug. He suddenly felt worn out, all his strength sapped. And he was terribly hungry and thirsty. He could not expect to find a house way out here in the middle of a forest, though, so he walked back out to where he thought he might find some people.

After a while he saw a small light twinkling in the distance. He walked fast toward the light, hoping that it would not prove to be the light of yet another tiger's eyes. No, it was a thatched hut. He called out, and a girl about seventeen came out. He could tell that no one else was around, and thought it was strange that she would be living in such a remote place all by herself. So he asked, "How is it that you are living alone way out here?"

"It may seem strange to you now, but if you listen to my story you will understand. I don't know how you came to be passing by here, but there is a cave not far from here. The big tiger living there took both my parents. So I built this thatched hut and live on grass and whatever else the forest gives me, waiting only for the day a person with a strong sense of righteousness comes along and helps me avenge my parents' death. You don't look like any ordinary sort. Would you be my champion?"

"Just you wait till I get my hands on that... By the way, where are we anyway?"

"This place is so remote no one has ever given it a name. But this is Kangwon Province and Hongch'ŏn is about sixty *ri* to the west."

"Are you telling me I ran several hundred *ri* tonight?"

"Did you really?"

Kwak rested the night there, and then, the next morning, he and his new friend went to the cave to wait for the tiger. But the tiger did not appear.

They sat down on a rock and started talking about what had happened the day before. Then at that moment the tiger approached slowly, with something in its mouth. When the tiger saw the two people it ran off. This time Kwak did not go after the tiger. He decided to wait for it to come back. So they waited, and waited, but the tiger did not return.

The girl then decided to go into the cave with a lantern. They groped about in the dim light for a long time, until finally they came upon an old couple sitting in a dark corner on a pile of soft dry grass. The girl dropped her lantern and ran to them and hugged them, bursting into tears. Kwak was dumbfounded.

Kwak thus learned that tigers are often more righteous than people. In those days, when the Koreans were being trampled by the Japanese and people often had to look out for themselves, they often found it necessary to hurt and deceive each other if they wanted to survive. This old man, the girl's father, had been prime minister and was very loyal to his nation and king. He was a man of great wisdom and ability, who could have become a pillar of strength to his ravaged country if it had not been for a snare woven by scheming villains in the court. He had been forced to return to his home town to live out the rest of his years in retirement.

But this tiger, sent by heaven to save him for later service to the nation, had taken the old couple to its cave. Now that some humans had come and broke into its cave, though, it had no choice but to leave the couple there and go away.

After this Kwak fought hard against the Japanese and before long obtained a high post in the government. The girl's father was also summoned back to the court by the King. He got back to work and rendered meritorious service to the King and the people.

Kwak and the girl, this couple brought together by the tiger, married and lived happily ever after. They never forgot their righteous tiger, who was able to recognize virtuous people and acted with all its might to protect them.

Yi Won-jo's Escape from the Tiger

Yi Won-jo, from Sŏngju in Kyŏngsang Province, was a minister to the court of King Ch'ŏlchong. His family was wealthy and had belonged to the gentry class for generations. His was a happy home, and the envy of others.

It had not always been so. For the longest time his father had no children. All his relatives were worried about him, wondering when he would have the male child that would continue their line. So his parents, getting desperate, decided to offer a hundred-day prayer. After deciding on the date and preparing the necessary things for the sacred rites, they climbed a mountain to perform the ceremony there. They finally came upon a huge flat rock on a grassy knoll towered over by high peaks, and decided to use this rock as an altar for the service. After performing their ablutions and placing the food on the rock, they prayed to the mountain spirit.

They prayed and prayed, pouring out their souls, until, before they knew it, a hundred days passed. On the last day, the one on which they would perform the concluding rites, they arranged everything and began a special prayer. But then, in the middle of this prayer,

Won-jo's father fell asleep. He dreamed that two white-haired old men had come out of a faint fog, and he listened to them.

"I'm starving to death. Man or spirit, one has to eat. No one can exist without food. Isn't there anything around here to eat?"

"Why, don't you see that table there, laden with all kinds of good food? Have that."

"Are you telling me to eat something that belongs to someone else? You know we can't eat it. Why do you go tempting me like that?"

"Are you so old you have forgotten who you are? It was prepared for you. Eat it and bless them with a child."

"But how can I bless them with a child when they are destined not to have one? Don't you understand these things? And I couldn't go borrow someone else's child, could I?"

"Oh, come on. Just cook up some magic. Then they'll be happy, and we can eat, so we'll be happy." He forced his friend to sit down in front of the table and kept urging him to eat.

"All right. I can't stand it, I'm so hungry. We'll finish this off and see what happens after." And he ate as much as he wanted, and then stood up and said, "Okay, let's get out of here."

"Where do you think you're going? You can't just eat somebody's food and not leave anything for it."

"I'm trapped now. I ate their food, knowing full well I shouldn't because I couldn't answer their prayers. So what else is there for me to do but get out of here as fast as I can?"

"Don't be so stubborn. There must be a child somewhere that you can give them. Even handicapped..."

"Well, come to think of it, there is one, a wonderfully formed one at that. But he is going to become a meal for a tiger when he reaches fifteen. It's better for him not to be born than to die young and break his parents' hearts. On the other hand, I guess I do owe them for the food I ate, so I guess I'd better give them this one."

After they finished their conversation they disappeared. When the childless father opened his eyes he realized he had been dreaming.

"That was quite a strange dream. If it comes true, the birth of the child will give me joy and his death will give me sorrow. So in the long run I'll be no better off than I am now." He did not even tell his wife about the dream, and remained silent as they packed their things and came down from the mountain.

In a short time his wife became pregnant and then gave birth to a boy. It was a great joy for the whole clan, infecting even the servants.

The child grew without mishap. He was very handsome and so intelligent that he could learn ten things for every one he was taught. And so, by the age of seven, he had mastered the Thousand Character text.

And then, in no time it seemed, he turned fifteen. There was a government civil service examination that year, and one of his father's cousins was departing for the capital to take the exam. This cousin told the boy's father, "That child of yours is so extraordinarily brilliant, and he's old enough to take the examination. Why not let him come with me and take the exam with me? It would be his first trip away from home, but since he'd be with me there wouldn't be any problem."

The boy's father thought deeply about his cousin's suggestion and decided that if a tiger had to get the boy it would be less painful to the family if it happened away from home. He knew he could not prevent the tiger from getting his son. After all, this was the will of heaven. But his wife did not want the child to go so far away and protested that he was too young. She was also worried that the child would be discouraged if he failed the examination. But her husband insisted.

After he sent the boy off, he sighed deeply, feeling as if he had sent him off to his death. "If he is taken by the tiger I will have lost my only child. Perhaps another hundred-day prayer would do some good." So he suggested this to his wife.

His wife, of course, asked him why the sudden concern, but he could not tell her the truth. "What's wrong with an extra prayer for the boy? Surely we can pray for him to take first place?" So she agreed.

They went back to that place where they had conducted their first hundred-day prayer. They prayed every night with all their hearts at the altar laden with food. While the boy's mother prayed that her son would take first place in the examination, the boy's father prayed for his son to escape the clutches of the tiger. And in this way a hundred days passed.

Again, as they were offering their last prayer, the father fell into a deep sleep. Soon he found himself in a stately mansion. In the middle of a huge room there was a brilliant throne and the King of Heaven was sitting on it. Civil and military officials, standing in two lines perpendicular to the throne, were listening to the King's words with the utmost deference.

"Who shall we declare as first on the examination list? I want your recommendations for the best one."

One official spoke up. "I would like to recommend the candidate from Sŏngju."

"He certainly did well, didn't he? Yes then, we will award him first place, if there are no objections."

At that moment another official said, "No, not him. What's the use of giving him first place when he is fated to be eaten by a tiger soon? I think we should give it to someone who can really benefit."

The father looked closely at the official who knew his son's fate, and saw that it was the white-haired old man from his previous dream.

The King of Heaven commanded his officials to summon the tiger. Shortly, a funny-looking man with a tiger-skin belt came in.

"Are you really going to eat that boy?" asked the King.

"Yes, of course I am," replied the tiger man.

"No. You must not eat him. He is the best candidate for first place on the state exam list. You can have a dog instead."

"No, I can't. It has already been decided that I am to

eat that boy."

"You impudent... How dare you go against my will." Then he told his Minister, "Call the hunter Wang in Kangwon Province to me."

Almost before the King's command was out of his mouth a short, stout hunter with a pockmarked face rushed in with his gun.

"Sure took you long enough. Anyway, shoot this scoundrel," the King ordered.

And then the boy's father was jolted awake by the blast of a gun. "Oh my lord, what a strange dream! Something like that first dream. Could it be possible that my Won-jo might come back safely, and with first place in the exam to boot?" And hoping against hope, the old man returned home.

After some time the news spread from Seoul throughout the whole country that Won-jo had placed first in the examination. His house was again overflowing with joy. Since he had passed the exam at an early age, not only his family but also the whole town of Sŏngju celebrated the boy's victory.

Soon Won-jo returned home. His traveling companion told his father, "Cousin, I had the strangest dream up in Seoul. The night before they announced the successful candidates in the examination I dreamed a huge tiger died. Some hunter shot it, right in front of the examination hall. When I awoke from my sleep something was urging me to go outside, so I went out in the yard and there was a tiger, big as a house, lying dead beside a short man with a gun. I asked him who he was, and he told me he was a hunter from Kangwon Province, and that he had come because he'd dreamed that some white-haired old man told him to go to Seoul as fast as he could and shoot a tiger he would find

Yi Won-jo's Escape from the Tiger

there. Now, doesn't that beat all!"

Won-jo's father smiled inside. Now he could stop worrying, and really enjoy his wonderful son.

Tiger as Divinities

A Righteous Tiger

Surrounding a tiny village in Chinyŏng County in North Chŏlla Province are mountains famous for the dense pine forests which are home to many tigers. One day a feast was given to celebrate the birthday of the richest man in the village.

A monk was passing by and heard the sounds of the clamorous celebration. He stopped to peer inside the house, and then just stood there shaking his head sadly.

Just then a young man carrying firewood on his back passed by the monk. The young man was so busy with his work, though, that he noticed neither the feast nor the monk. But he heard the monk when the monk called him.

"Young man, do you live in this village?"

"Yes, I do."

"Well I'd like to ask you something then. Is there a son in this house?"

"Why do you want to know?"

"Never mind why I want to know. But I can tell you that something unspeakably horrible is going to happen. Listen, would you do me a favor? It's getting dark, and I'm on a long journey. Can I spend the night at your place?"

The woodcutter hesitated because he was living with his mother in a tiny, ramshackle hut. But he could not refuse the old monk's request. "It's awfully uncomfortable at my place, but you're welcome to stay."

After dinner they talked about many things with open hearts, and then the woodcutter remembered what the old monk had told him before. "Honorable monk, if I ask you a question will you please be frank with me?"

"Ask me anything you want."

"Would you explain what you told me in front of that rich man's house before?"

"But I've told you already, it is something I can't utter, not to a soul. The more you know, the more you will suffer."

With this, of course, the woodcutter became all the more curious. "Honorable monk, it is said that even if our sleeve only brushes against another's it is something meant to be. Here we are spending the night together, close enough already to be opening our hearts to each other like this. Why do you hesitate to tell me? It may be important, but nothing can be so important that you can't trust me with it."

The monk considered this, and then said, "You must keep it a secret then."

"I've guessed that much."

"If you don't, you will be the one misfortune hits."

"I understand. Please tell me."

"After five days calamity is going to befall the rich man's family, something nobody would ever dream could happen. Their only son is going to be killed by a tiger."

The young man was puzzled. The monk warned him again, solemnly, "If you let them know, you'll be the victim instead of the boy. Be very careful not to say a thing, to anyone."

"But can this really be true?"

"You will see soon enough. Everyone will see."

The woodcutter became worried more now about the boy's fate than about his own. Wasn't there some way to prevent it? "Please tell me how we can prevent this. I mean, if you know it's going to happen you must also know a way to keep it from happening."

"There is a way, of course. But I can tell it to no one, because whoever discloses the secret will become the victim." The monk showed he did not want to discuss this any further.

The woodcutter was a very kindhearted young man, and he wanted to save the boy's life. So he asked the monk again, "Please tell me how to save him."

"No."

"Please. I'll take whatever punishment you would get for letting out the secret."

"You are a good man. I guess I should be at least that good, seeing as I'm a monk. All right then. The only way is to cut down a few pine trees and make a high pile with them, and put the child on it. Then the boy can be saved."

When the woodcutter woke up the next morning the monk was gone. He thought about all the monk had told him, and then shuddered at the thought, "Could this old monk actually be a tiger himself?"

The young man did not know what to do with himself from the day he heard the old monk's secret. His conscience hurt him because, though he knew what was going to happen and how to prevent it, he was unable to get himself to do anything for fear this thing might really happen to himself, like the monk had warned. As each day passed he fretted more and lost sleep and grew thin from not being able to eat. How true that old saying is, that once you learn of someone's misfortune it becomes your own.

Then one night he had a dream in which he was chased by a tiger. He came to a cave where he could escape the tiger, but at that moment the rich man's son blocked his way and kept him out of the cave. The woodcutter told the boy he was being chased by a tiger and begged the boy to save him. He was begging and weeping even when he woke out of the dream. The nightmare stopped, but the anguish continued.

"The boy is going to die tomorrow, I'm sure. This is the good spirit's way of telling me to save the boy's life before it's too late. I'll go to the boy's family and tell them the secret, whatever finally happens to me. But no, no, I don't want to die in his place. And then there's Mother. How will she ever get by without me?" Conscience and dread pulled his heart two ways, and he could not make up his mind. "But then, if I give my life for his son the rich man will take care of my mother after I'm gone. Maybe that would be better for her, because then she would lead a much more comfortable life than the one I've provided her."

So the next day he was off to the rich man's house, but with a very heavy heart. He hesitated when he reached the front gate of the huge house. Then, drawing all the courage he could from his whole being, he knocked and was soon inside. The rich man was an arrogant man, but the woodcutter did not let this stop him from telling the whole story, from beginning to end.

The man shuddered, as if he saw his own death approaching. But then he recovered and scoffed, "What a crazy story! My son taken away by a tiger? What is it you want from me? Why are you telling me such a ridiculous story? Out of rice? You want money?"

Though the man sneered at the young woodcutter, his wife believed him. "The young man has no reason at all to go around saying such things if they're not true. He is well known through the whole village for his honesty. Now let's do what he says. It's better to be safe than sorry."

So, at his wife's behest the master ordered the servants to cut down some pine trees and pile them high in the yard. By sunset the pile stood higher than the roof. And the whole family waited.

Throughout the night the villagers huddled in their homes in fear of their lives. But then, at daybreak, everyone was relieved to hear the noisy chatter of the magpies. At midday the village was perfectly still, and not even the mew of a cat, let alone the roar of a tiger, could be heard. So they started complaining about the woodcutter.

The rich man, who had not slept a wink that night and was even grouchier than ever, called the young woodcutter in front of him. "Just like they say. It's the one that you trust most that will betray you first. How dare you tell such a dreadful lie!" But his only son was still troubled and his wife was still beside herself in anxiety, so they decided to put their son on the pile one more night.

Again the sun set and the villagers were just starting to leave the rich man's house for their homes when, with a thunderous roar, a huge tiger jumped over the garden wall. Everybody scattered. Only the family of the boy stayed put, in the house. The tiger stared at the pile for a long while, then howled with anger and des-

A Righteous Tiger

peration. Its eyes glowed like fire and every hair on its body bristled like needles. It tried to jump the pile, but the pile was too high. And then the tiger gave a snort of disgust, and disappeared like a bolt of lightening over the garden wall.

And so the rich man's son was saved. His father was overcome with joy and gratitude. He called the young man to him. "How can I express my gratitude to you? If there is anything you want, please don't hesitate. Tell me, right now, and I'll do whatever I can for you."

Nothing, though, could change the young woodcutter's fate. He merely said, "I don't need anything. But if some misfortune befalls me, I wish you would take care of my mother. She's got no one but me, you see. If you would do this I would be very grateful."

"What are you talking about? What kind of misfortune would befall a nice young man like you?"

Time passed. The numerous versions that people had invented of the tiger story all faded from memory. The woodcutter, though, spent every day in fear for his life.

Soon he couldn't take anymore. One day he climbed the mountain to look for a proper place to wait for the tiger to come and take him, and get it over with. He sat down and waited, heaving sigh after sigh. Before long, sure enough, the tiger appeared. Though he had thought endlessly about this moment for the last several months, he was not prepared for this. He was as terrified as if he had never given the tiger a thought. The young man stayed where he was, though, because he knew it would be useless to try to avoid his fate.

"So, at long last. Didn't I warn you that night not to reveal the secret? Didn't I warn you that you'd die in the boy's place? Because of you I missed the chance to transform myself into a human being. And now I'm going to get my revenge. Eating you won't help me become a human, but it will give me the satisfaction of doing away with my arch enemy."

"Go on then. I broke the promise I made to you, so I have to die. But as a human I do have a conscience, something you animals aren't burdened with, and sometimes it makes us give up things we want, even our life. I tried, but I couldn't live any longer with that guilty conscience. So I did what I had to do. And now my life is at your disposal. Maybe it's better now, while I have a clean conscience."

"You really are a remarkable young man. You know, most of your kind are nothing in comparison with you, not even a shadow of you. They're worth less than dogs and pigs. Sure, they talk about conscience all the time, even though they have none, and despise others for behaving as they themselves do. Well, I may be just an animal, but among animals I'm as intelligent as you can get. Might say even philosophical on occasion. So I guess I'll have to let you go. I couldn't hurt someone with as noble a heart as you have. Go on, get out of here, back to your mother. And you keep on taking good care of her, you hear? And you keep that nice clean conscience, too, or else..."

With that the tiger disappeared, like the wind. And the young woodcutter was able to live a long and happy life.

A Hair from the Tiger's Eyebrow

There once lived a farmer named Sŏk Yong-p'al. He had such a good nature that he did not know even the meaning of the word "evil." Unfortunately, he was just as poor as he was good.

He worked very hard in the field from sunrise to sunset. No matter how hard he worked, though, his poverty meant he frequently had to skip meals. He considered himself lucky when he was able to manage a bowl of barley porridge.

Though his life was difficult, he worked diligently with the hope that someday fate would smile on him. But his wife, nearing forty, had not produced any children, and only a chilly loneliness filled his house. To make matters worse, this wife of his was ill-tempered and cold-hearted, and she tormented him constantly. She got so bad he was sometimes afraid of living in such a world.

One day when Yong-p'al returned home from the field his wife, instead of giving him the dinner he was so hungry for, gave him a strong dose of abuse.

"What are you doing every day like this, not even managing to support your wife? What kind of a man are you? And if you keep walking around with that hang-dog look on that ugly mug of yours you might as well just kill yourself and be done with all your problems."

Yong-p'al was deeply hurt by his wife's hatred and contempt. But he was so accustomed to these harangues that, as usual, he did not say a single word in reply.

His silence made his wife even angrier. "Well why don't you say something? You worthless... And what are you going to do about getting some food in this house? Can't you do anything but go out and waste your time in those fields all day long?"

But he said nothing. Now she was furious. "Why do you act like such an imbecile? Why can't you accomplish something? Don't just stand there like some statue. Oh, I can't endure this life with you any longer. Get out! Go on, get out of my house!" And she pushed him out of the house.

Outside, the moon, as if trying to be of some comfort to him, shone brightly on him. But it was of no comfort to the hungry Yong-p'al, who had no place to go. Where around here could he get some food to stop the constant grumbling of his stomach? Nowhere. Where could he find rest? Not around here. His tears sparkled in the moonlight.

After mulling over where he could go, Yong-p'al finally decided to spend the night at Tiger Rock. They said that in ancient times a tiger used to come and cry at this rock every first full moon of the year. Now, though, it was a favorite place for the kids in the village to play.

Yong-p'al went into the woods and found the rock. He sat down on the ground and leaned against the rock, and sighed deeply over and over as he watched the waning moon. But then a rustling sound drew his attention to a nearby tree. An old monk was sitting there, picking lice out of his clothes and popping them in his mouth. Yong-p'al thought the monk might be a ghost; no living human would be catching lice in the middle of the night out here in the middle of nowhere. But then he wondered whether the monk might not just be in the same situation he was. So he cautiously approached the old monk and asked, "I beg your pardon, but what brings you out to the woods like this, at this time of night?"

The monk slowly straightened his trousers, then turned to Yong-p'al and said, "What I'm doing here is my business. So what are you doing here?"

Yong-p'al told him his life story and what had happened with his wife that night. "I have no wish to live with her any longer. In fact, I have no wish to live at all."

The monk smiled at him. Then he pulled a hair from his eyebrow, gave it to Yong-p'al, and told him to hold it up to his eye. Puzzled, Yong-p'al did as he was told. What he saw then stunned him so that he almost keeled over. Instead of an old monk, there was a huge tiger, the size of a mountain, with its mouth wide open and ready to devour Yong-p'al in one gulp. Yong-p'al quickly pulled the hair down from his eye, and there was the smiling old monk again.

"Yes, I'm actually a tiger, from T'aebaek Mountain. I came out this way for a nice walk, but I became hungry and I'm looking for some food now. You know what spiritual creatures we tigers are, so you don't have to be afraid of becoming my meal. You're a human, so I can't eat you. It's only those so-called humans that are actually dogs and pigs and other low-lifes that we tigers can eat. You know, in this world there are not really that

A Hair from the Tiger's Eyebrow   155

many real humans at all.

"Take your wife, now. She's produced no offspring for you, she's ill-tempered. The only thing she's ever given you is a lousy life. She could be either a pig or maybe a dog. That type makes others' lives miserable. Here, take this hair from my eyebrow and go back to your house and look at your wife through it. Now, if she turns out to be an animal, go straight to Aji Village, on P'algong Mountain. There you will find a widow living in a hut under a big pine tree. Tell her what I just told you, and take her as your new wife. Then, I promise, you will prosper and be happy."

Now it was getting light, and the farmers of the village were already coming out to the woods for some firewood. The monk told Yong-p'al to get going, because he had some business to attend to.

Yong-p'al thanked the monk and started back to his house. When he thought the monk could not see him, though, he hid behind a tree and watched him. He had already turned himself back into a tiger. The tiger ran over to the men coming into the woods, and carried off one of them. Yong-p'al turned and high-tailed it out of there.

As soon as he got back home he looked at his wife through the hair from the tiger's eyebrow. What a sight! Instead of his wife he saw a fat sleeping sow, slobbering and snoring in a bad dream.

He didn't even stop to say good-bye, and took off for Aji Village. At dusk, after three days' walk he arrived at the hut under the pine trees that the monk told him to look for. He called several times for someone to come to the door, but there was no response. Finally, he pushed open the gate and went in. He found a woman sleeping.

She was awakened when the floor creaked under his

weight, and she screamed, "A man! Who are you! How dare you enter a house where a woman is living all by herself!"

Yong-p'al apologized profusely, and then he explained why he came. When the woman finally understood, she welcomed him. Then she told him her story.

"After I got married life turned bad. My husband was a philanderer, always out every night with any and every girl he could find. Then one day he just up and disappeared. And ever since then I've been living by myself."

"Looks like we're in the same boat now."

"You know, when you came in I was having a really strange dream. Some old man with a snowy white beard and glowing face told me that a stranger would come here, and that he would be my true husband. And that if I honored and served him well I would have a happy life from then on. Then the old man disappeared, and as soon as I woke up there you were."

Naturally, Yong-p'al and the woman married. They lived in her house, and worked very hard together. And they did indeed have a happy life together. In fact, she gave birth to a healthy baby boy. The family spent each day with joy and laughter.

One autumn day Yong-p'al packed a bag and started on a journey to Songdo, the capital city, which he had always wanted to visit. On the way he passed through a village and, as it was getting dark, went to the marketplace to see if he could find a place to sleep. Farmers with their heavy burdens on their backs were returning from their work in the fields. Yong-p'al watched them through his tiger's hair and found some of them to be animals. He spent the night at a farmer's house and continued on his journey.

After fifteen days he finally entered the capital city. It was crowded, and splendid. He felt as if he were in paradise. The people in the streets were dressed in gorgeous clothes, and the wind chimes hanging from the eaves of the huge tile-roofed houses clanged merrily. Yong-p'al was overwhelmed with the splendor of the city. When it grew dark, he knocked at the gate of one of the big houses that had impressed him so, and asked a servant if he could spend the night there.

"Go somewhere else, quick! My master is a real terror, and if he hears you here there'll be no end of trouble. Go on, get!"

But Yong-p'al persisted, mainly because he did not like this kind of treatment. Then the master heard them and came stomping out to the front door. He yelled, "What's that beggar making all that noise for in my house? Throw him out. Now!"

Yong-p'al, of course, was dying to try his tiger's hair on this master. So he brought it up to his eye and took a look. Sure enough, an oily pig was rutting on the floor for food.

So Yong-p'al spent the night beside a fence. From early in the morning he entertained himself by watching the hurrying passers-by through his tiger's eyebrow hair. Here a pig dressed in splendid clothes sitting in a sedan chair ordering his servants around. There a fox, and over there another pig. He was hardly able to see a human among them.

That night he again had trouble finding a place to sleep. Then he saw a poorly dressed man and asked him if he could stay with him. The man kindly agreed.

The man and his wife gave Yong-p'al a sparse but decent meal. After dinner Yong-p'al chatted with the man while the small son of the house played in his lap.

Yong-p'al had already found that this man was genuine, so he expected the son to be too. But when he looked at the son through the tiger's hair, he was surprised to find a puppy with curly hair.

Greatly saddened, he heaved a deep sigh. The man asked him what was wrong. "Are you uncomfortable? Is it something we've done?"

Yong-p'al had to tell the kind man what was bothering him. "When I saw your son he appeared as a puppy. That's why I sighed."

The man pleaded with Yong-p'al to save his only son. "He's the last in a long line of only sons. All our hopes hang on him. If something happens to him it will kill me sure as if it happened to myself."

Yong-p'al did not know what to do. But then he remembered the spirit which appeared in his wife's dream, the mountain spirit. On each mountain there lives a mountain spirit that governs all the animals on that mountain. Yong-p'al thought the spirit might help if they prayed to it. So he advised the man to perform a rite to the mountain spirit.

The man thought this was a wonderful idea, and asked Yong-p'al, "But where should I perform the rite?"

"The tiger I met told me he lives in Musa Valley, in T'aebaek Mountain. How about trying there?"

The next day they prepared a large sack of rice cakes and set off for Musa Valley. After fifteen days of walking they arrived at the valley. They conducted the rite and offered the rice cakes. On the second day they did the same. Then, on the third day, at three in the morning, the mountain spirit with his long white beard appeared before them.

"Your son was destined to die, quite soon in fact. But, because of your devotion, I will grant your request.

Now in this country, there is only one adult tiger left. When General Kang Kam-ch'an drove all the tigers into Manchuria this particular tiger was pregnant and couldn't make it across the Yalu. So the General took pity on it and allowed it to stay here. That is the very tiger we have in Musa Valley. Now, I've promised I'll save your son, so I'm going to have to make the tiger blind. As long as you live the tiger will not harm your son. But you must remember that your son is actually a dog, and when you die your wish dies with you. When you're gone the tiger's offspring will take away your son. That is his fate, and that I cannot change."

Then the mountain spirit disappeared. Soon after, the old monk whom Yong-p'al had met appeared. From his blind eyes flowed tears of grief at his great misfortune. "Now in my ripe old age I have become blind. What will happen to my poor children? I love my children as much as you love yours. I too want to raise them to healthy adults. But how can I hunt and feed them without my sight? Please help me. Let me have my sight back. As long as I live I will make sure my cubs don't harm your son. Please, write a petition to the mountain spirit to give me back my sight." And he knelt down and wept.

Yong-p'al felt sorry for the old monk. He remembered the help the monk had given, so he asked the man to write a petition and put it on the rock where the mountain spirit had appeared.

The old tiger did get its sight back, and the man's son grew up to have a son of his own.

But after many years passed the man grew old, and the tiger grew older. The man died, and on the first anniversary of the man's death the tiger died. And on that day the tiger's offspring delivered the man's son his fate.

Tips for Catching Tiger

Fighting Tiger with Fire

Once there lived a woodcutter deep in the mountains. He had no family to support but, being a woodcutter, his life was by no means an easy one. He cut twigs and boughs all day long but barely earned enough to buy food for three meals a day, let alone for storing up for a rainy day.

So on days when he could not work he simply had to go without food. On a good day he would catch a rabbit, maybe a small deer, but on days when his luck was not so good he might encounter a bear or a boar and have to run back home, abandoning not only any food he had caught but even his wood and A-frame. So he counted himself lucky on those days he was able to gather enough wood to bring in the grain for three meals.

Our story starts in the early winter, which is a busy time in the mountains for both woodcutters and farmers, who are then gathering wood for winter fuel. It was a chilly, overcast day. The woodcutter climbed way up the mountain to cut some logs. He was shivering because a chilly wind was stealing through his thin trousers.

At the summit of the mountain the woodcutter took

off his A-frame and began chopping down a tree. Before he was able to chop it all the way down, though, he heard some rustling in the hazel trees in back of him, so he looked around to see what was causing it. There stood a huge tiger, glaring at him. An ordinary man would have fainted right on the spot, but our woodcutter was used to encounters with wild beasts. He kept his wits about him, trying to figure a way to escape. There was no place nearby for him to shelter himself, so he had no choice but to fight.

He faced the tiger squarely, and lifted his ax with his trembling arms. The tiger approached slowly, but confidently, staring him straight in the eye. The woodcutter's legs began to wobble, but then he got an idea. Knowing that tigers cannot climb trees, he turned quickly to the tree he had been chopping at and nimbly scaled it.

The tiger leaped up at him several times, trying to catch hold of him. But the woodcutter was at the top of the tree by now, out of reach. So the tiger laid a siege, and the two waited to see which would tire first.

The woodcutter knew he had to figure out a way to kill this tiger, who seemed content to wait there till kingdom come. It occurred to him that although his trousers had no lining his jacket was padded with cotton wool. He began breaking twigs off the tree and throwing them down to the ground.

Now a tiger is not stupid, and this tiger pushed every twig under his haunches, knowing that if the man kept this up long enough it would eventually be raised to the same level as the man.

When the woodcutter thought the pile under the tiger had enough twigs in it he pulled the cotton wool padding from his jacket, kept a small ball of it, and threw the rest down at the tiger. The tiger pushed that under his haunches as well. Then the man got out his flint and lit the cotton wool he had kept, and threw the cotton-wool ball down at a piece of his lining sticking out from under the tiger's haunches. The pile beneath the tiger burst into flames and the tiger's fur caught fire. It began to run away, but of course this only made his fur burn faster. And needless to say, that was the end of this tiger.

So the woodcutter came home with a nice big tiger on his A-frame.

The New Mother and the Insatiable Tiger

A charcoal seller and his wife once lived a little down the mountain from the Chŏngŭp Mountain Fortress. There was not a neighbor within 10 *ri*.

The wife was expecting, and her heavy body made it difficult for her to get around. Her husband was concerned about her and helped as much as he could, but there were times that other things came first. One day, for example, he told her, leaving for the market, "I don't like leaving you alone like this, but if I don't go you won't get any food. You'd like some laver and soy sauce now, wouldn't you? I'll try to get back tonight, no matter how late."

When he got to the market the sky blackened suddenly with heavy clouds, and the rain was soon coming down in buckets. The rain kept everyone indoors, so he could not sell his charcoal. He had to go from house to house to peddle his charcoal, which exhausted him so much he had no strength to return home. Besides, he had no food to bring back with him because the rain had forced all the market vendors to pack up and go home by the time he had sold enough charcoal to buy anything.

As tired as he was, he would have spent the night in town. But his expectant wife probably needed him, so he set out for home with lots of charcoal and none of the supplies he had traveled all that way to buy.

While he was struggling back over hill and mountain his wife gave birth to a baby boy. The birth was easy, but she was very hungry. There was nothing to eat in the house except a little rice, so the wife decided to cook some rice gruel for herself.

She went out around the house to the fireplace in the lean-to where she did her cooking, and discovered that when she was giving birth to her baby their dog was also giving birth to three puppies.

She was bent over the pot when suddenly she heard a deep growl in back of her, at the edge of their clearing. She turned and saw a very hungry-looking tiger coming toward her, slowly but all too fast for her.

The woman stood up, looked in the dog's eyes, patted its head, and said, "I know you love your pups, just as much as I love my baby. Mother's love is mother's love. But your pups are animals and my baby's a human, so I'm pulling rank on you. I'm sorry, but I'm going to have to ask you to understand." With that, she picked up one of the pups and threw it to the approaching tiger. "Here! Now go back home."

The tiger caught the pup in his mouth and the pup was in the tiger's stomach almost before he had time to swallow it.

"Must be starving!" She picked up another pup and tossed this one to the tiger too. It disappeared just as fast as the first one. And the tiger just stood there, waiting for more.

"This simply will not do," the woman thought to her-

The New Mother and the Insatiable Tiger   169

self. "One pup was bad enough, but two pups... And now he wants another! The more he gets, the more he wants, and I'm just whetting his appetite with these poor pups. No more of that. We'll just have to trick the greedy beast."

The woman wrapped some cotton around a couple hot stones from the fireplace, in a ball about the size of one of the pups, then threw the ball to the tiger. The tiger gulped this one down just like the first two. U-m-m-m, good!

Bad! The tiger was soon running around like mad, trying to do something about the horrible pain in his stomach. Then merciful death came.

The woman's husband returned early the next morning, empty-handed. To his great surprise there was a big dead tiger waiting for him in the yard, and a healthy mother and child waiting for him in his house.

That day he went back and reported the incident with the tiger to the government office in town, and received a nice reward of a bag of rice, some laver and, to top it off, some soy sauce.

Fifty-Man Pass

The Kari Mountains' Fifty-Man Pass, in Kimp'o County, is the longest and steepest of all in Kyŏnggi Province. And in those days it was so remote and wild that tigers used to prey on travelers even during the brightest hours of the day.

People used to form in groups of fifty to cross this pass. A traveller would put up at the inn at the foot of the pass until forty-nine more came along, and then all of them would cross the pass together. They carried torches and played gongs and drums to scare off the tigers. The tigers would watch the group go by, and the people would talk later of how they could see the tigers' eyes through the trees, burning like fireballs.

One day a bushy-haired young man appeared at the roadhouse and asked for something to drink. After draining several bowls of rice brew he stood up and said he was going to cross the pass all by himself. There were several others who had been waiting for a group of fifty to accumulate, and when they heard this young man they wondered about his sanity. All alone, and he did not even have a weapon!

They tried to dissuade him, but he just jeered them for their timidity and set out alone. They felt sorry for the young man, because he did not have a chance. But then, when they considered his arrogant bravado and recklessness, they thought maybe he deserved to get a good lesson.

Not long after the young man left several men arrived together at the inn. Now they had enough for a group of fifty, so they left the inn and headed up the pass, torches glaring and drums banging. When they got to the top of the pass they heard the mighty roar of a tiger even above their noisy banging. They stopped and looked around to find out what was going on.

Then they just barely made out the dim silhouette of two figures struggling with each other. The bunch got closer and discovered that the two figures were the young man and a tiger in mortal combat. The young man had the tiger fast by its tail, and the tiger was trying to grab the young man in its jaws. But the young man danced so agilely away from the tiger's thrusts that no matter how the tiger strained it could not catch the young man.

The tiger ran up the slope to somehow shake off the young man, but the young man kept his tight grip on its tail, and finally dragged the tiger back on down the slope when the tiger exhausted itself. But then the tiger would regain some of his energy and bound up the slope again, then get tired and come back down with the young man.

After several rounds of this, the tiger and the young man both dropped from exhaustion. So the men ran up and pummeled the tiger to death with their clubs.

It so happens that the tiger the young man took on was king of the tigers in that mountain pass. Seeing their king beaten to death, the other tigers moved deep into the forest, and eventually ended up on another range. So, thanks to the fearless young man with the bushy hair and arrogant confidence, from that time on people have been able to cross Fifty-Man Pass alone, without any fear.

Tiger and Juju

Once upon a time there was a young mother with a brand new baby. She had to finish sewing something for her husband, and wanted the baby to go to sleep. So the mother picked up the baby and began to suckle it, but the baby did not want to sleep and just kept crying and fretting.

So she said to the baby, "Look, honey, if you don't go to sleep a tiger will come and carry you away. In fact, there's a tiger outside our door right now, looking in here to see if there is a naughty baby around."

But the baby just kept on crying, as if it did not care at all what any tiger might try to do. The frustrated mother then raised her voice and said, "Okay, okay. Look, here's a juju for you." And the baby became quiet.

Well, it just so happened that a tiger, just down from the mountain, was indeed listening at the door. And it was not happy, not at all. It had always prided itself on being the most terrifying creature on the face of the earth, and was now being shown that there was some other creature named Juju apparently far more terrifying than itself. This would not do. It regretted having lost touch with the world by staying in the mountains too much.

The tiger decided, though, that his hunger hurt a lot more than his hurt pride, so he crept round to the cow shed to satisfy his hunger with a calf. Stealthily it moved into the darkness of the shed.

Just then the young woman's husband returned home from visiting a friend. He remembered the new calf and went back to the cow shed to wrap up the young creature against the cold with a straw mat. He walked into the quiet shack and found the mat. The tiger, hiding in the shadows, still had Juju on his mind, and thought this must be Juju who just walked in. Juju was coming to get him! And sure enough, Juju walked over to the tiger and put the mat over him.

The tiger panicked and tried to run. But the man could not let his nice new calf get loose, so he grabbed the tiger and jumped on its back. This scared the tiger even more, and he burst out of the shack and ran as fast as his legs would carry him, back up the mountain.

The animal ran all night with the man on his back. When day dawned, the man finally noticed that this was not a surprisingly strong calf but a tiger. The man's every muscle stiffened in fright, and he would have fallen off the tiger if he were not petrified.

Soon he started trying to collect himself, and he finally realized that if the tiger took him to his den it would be all over for him. Then he saw a branch hanging from a huge dead tree looming in front of them. As the tiger ran under the branch, the man jumped off the tiger and grabbed hold of the branch. Then he scrambled higher up the tree.

The tiger, noticing the weight gone from his back, stopped. He was still scared, but felt an irresistible urge to see what Juju looked like. It was not only curiosity—he would have to know what Juju looked like so he could avoid him next time. So he looked back cautiously, but saw nothing. He looked all around, and then finally spied something up in the dead tree. That was no Juju. It was just a man.

The tiger was furious. He was also hungry. So he decided to make a meal of the man. But what could he do? Tigers can not climb trees.

He would have to call his brethren for some help, and so he bounded off into the trees. The man saw this and wondered whether he should climb down and run back home. But he decided not to because the tiger might be hiding behind some tree in ambush.

By and by he saw a band of tigers bounding through the forest in his direction. He knew he was finished. The tigers screeched to a stop at the bottom of the tree, and held a conference among themselves. Then the biggest and strongest of them crouched at the bottom of the tree and another tiger climbed on its back. And another tiger climbed up on this one's back. They were getting close, so the man climbed higher. Then another climbed on the last tiger's back, and another one on this one. The man climbed higher. And it went on this way till the man got to the top of the tree.

There were lots more tigers left, but no more tree.

The man gave up all hope. This was it. So he decided to play a song to try to calm himself and give himself some semblance of dignity in the last moments of his life. He broke off a twig, twisted its bark loose, and began to blow on the hollow pipe. He kept his eyes off the approaching tigers and played with all his heart and soul.

Then the tiger at the very bottom of the tower began to dance. You see, it had just eaten a shaman. As this tiger gyrated wildly, the tigers on top all fell to the ground in a heap. The man opened his eyes when he heard the fuss. There were a score of tigers scattered all over the ground, some with broken ribs, some with cracked skulls, and some with broken limbs.

He climbed down the tree, stepped gingerly out through the writhing tigers, and dashed on home. Then he rounded up some of his friends and brought them back to the site of the massacre. And he and his friends lived prosperous lives on the money they got from all those tiger skins.

The Salt Peddler and the Monk

If you are on foot, Kangwon Province, with its steep and densely wooded hills and mountains inhabited by all sorts of wild animals, is not a place you want to be by yourself. This story will show you how perilous it can be.

Once upon a time a salt peddler had to go over Taegwallyŏng Pass, the steepest of those very steep passes in the T'aebaek Range. He climbed to the top with difficulty, removed his A-frame, and sat down on a tree trunk to catch his breath.

Just then a huge tiger jumped out from behind a tree. In panic the man grabbed hold of the tiger's tail. A tiger cannot bend back around, so it was helpless as long as the man could hold on. It strained and writhed to get away, but the peddler held on for dear life.

Soon a young monk came up the pass, his grey robe flapping in the wind. This was years ago, when Buddhism was at its nadir. It had lost its official status as the national religion and had also lost its popularity with the people because it was corrupt and degenerate. So monks were treated as pariahs. Buddhist temples had moved into remote mountains and monks avoided well-travelled thoroughfares, sticking to back alleys in

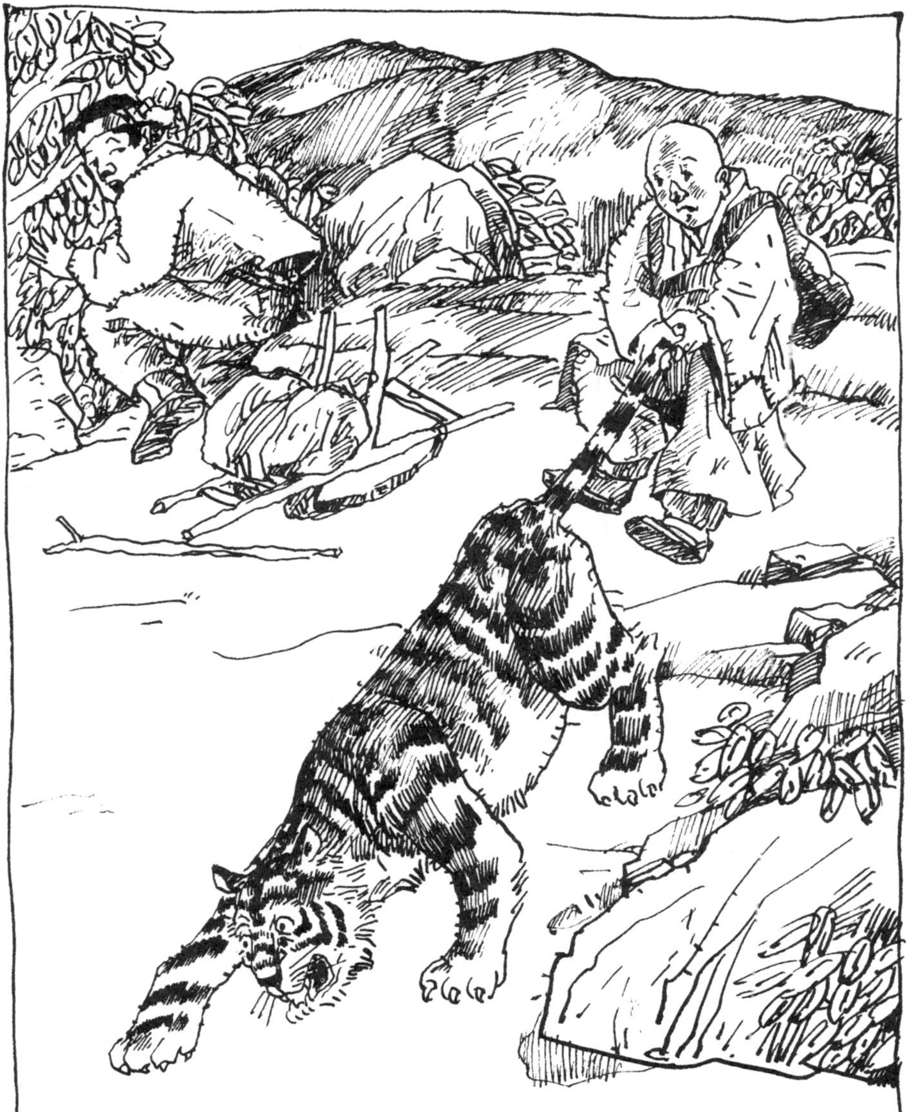

the cities and deserted trails out in the countryside.

When the peddler saw the monk he felt Providence was watching over him. As he struggled to hold on to the tiger he grunted a "na-mu-a-mi-ta-bul" in thanks to the Buddha, then called to the monk imperiously, "You, come here!"

"Your humble servant, sir," replied the monk, approaching but keeping his distance of the lurching tiger.

"As you can see I've got my hands full here. I'm trying to subdue this guy, but it looks like it's going to take a bit longer. And wouldn't you know it, I have to take a piss. Come here and hold on while I see to my business, then we'll kill the thing and share what we get for the skin."

The monk beamed with delight. "As you wish, sir," and he grabbed the tiger's tail. "All right, go ahead and relieve yourself. Don't worry—I'll hold on till you get back."

The peddler ran into the trees. But what he relieved himself of was not what the monk had in mind, because he just kept on running. He did not even care about his A-frame, he was so happy to get out of there. "A monk's *karma* is no business of mine," he thought to himself, and he hurried on.

But his conscience started bothering him, and it got worse and worse and would not let up for three years. It bothered him so badly he decided to go back to that pass where he had left the monk.

On the way up the pass he worried whether that tiger might be there waiting for him, or the monk's ghost might come and haunt him. But when he reached the spot he could not believe his eyes. The monk was still holding that same tiger by the tail, just as he was three years ago.

"But what are you two doing still here after all this time?"

"Well, after you went to relieve yourself," he grunted as his foe jerked hard, "the tiger began to strain and pull even harder, so there was nothing I could do but let it drag me along. I've toured all eight provinces three times like this, and just got back here today. If you had taken longer relieving yourself you'd have missed me because we'd have gone off on our fourth tour. Here, take the tail now."

The peddler stood there dumbfounded. Just then the tiger began to put up a terrific battle, so the peddler took out his knife and killed it. Then he and the monk skinned the tiger and brought the skin to the market in the nearest town. They sold the skin and split the money.

With this the peddler had enough money to stop peddling salt for a living, and the monk could afford to grow his hair back and live the life of an ordinary man.

Human Tiger Bait

Many years ago there lived a salt peddler. Once he had been trying all day long to cross a mountain, but the sun set before he could accomplish this. He looked for a shack or a cave where he could pass the night, and finally spotted a dim light in the distance.

When he got to the hut he found just one man living there all by himself. The man kindly offered to let the peddler stay the night. Exhausted from walking all day, the peddler fell asleep almost before he got his thank you out of his mouth.

During the night, though, the peddler woke with a start. He found himself in a huge net, together with a big piece of rice cake. And there beside the net was his host. He knew there was no use shouting for help way out here in the middle of nowhere, so he just looked at his host. At the same time he was thinking, "I should have known something was up with this guy living here all by himself in this lonely mountain. So what is he? A ghost? A fox turned human? A robber? And what plans has he got for me? Well, maybe it's all the same: I'd have been eaten by a tiger anyway if I had slept outside, so I guess I'm no worse off." And he resigned himself to his fate.

The host shouldered his bundle and took it even higher up the mountain. The peddler thought his host must surely be a fox, since a robber would just take his money and leave him there to die or whatever.

After a while they came to a large dead tree. The peddler's host hung the net from a high limb and disappeared into the night, without even a good-bye.

"Now, what kind of nonsense is this? A fox would have eaten me, a robber would rob me. But he just leaves me hanging here. Am I supposed to be a sacrifice to the tree spirit?"

It was not long before tigers were gathering around the tree. They whispered among themselves, wondering where that juicy, tempting human smell was coming from. Then they spotted the human dangling up in the tree, and one leaped to catch him in its jaws. The human was just a bit too high. And then the tiger disappeared. Another tiger tried the same thing, and this one also disappeared. Tiger after tiger disappeared into the deep pond at the foot of the tree.

After all the tigers were drowned in the pond, the host came out from his hiding place. He drew down the net and opened it. "I'm sorry I had to use you like this. I used to be a merchant with a very profitable business, but someone swindled me and I lost everything. Then my creditors got after me, so I couldn't stay in town anymore, and I came out here. When I saw you I got the idea that I could catch a few tigers with you. I'll share the profits, don't worry. Can you forgive me?"

We do not know whether his bait forgave him. We do know, though, that the two men split the proceeds and lived the rest of their days in comfort.

184 *Tiger, Burning Bright*

Greased Puppy

There were two brothers who always got along together very well. But then, after their parents died, the older brother showed his real nature. He became covetous of the inheritance the parents had left and tried to get it all for himself. So he drove his younger brother out of the house and forbade him to ever even come near the place. In those days the eldest brother could do things like that.

The villagers took pity on the younger brother and gave him a small plot of land to till for his family. It was barren land, though, not really fit for growing grain. So the younger brother decided he would have to plant sesame.

He went to his brother to ask for some sesame seeds. Of course, the older brother was angry that this younger brother had returned after he had told him never to come back. What made him even angrier, though, was the fact that his younger brother had some land. So he gave him boiled sesame seeds, which are useless for growing anything.

The younger brother did not know that his older brother was tricking him, so, bowing again and again he thanked him profusely, and then went back home.

There he carefully planted the seeds.

Heaven was kind to him, and it turned out that one of the seeds had not been boiled. This seed sprouted and grew into a huge bush with branches that spread wide in every direction. The younger brother tended it devotedly, and the tree yielded an abundant supply of sesame seeds. At harvest time the bush was so big that the neighbors had to come and help him cut the branches off and gather all the seeds.

The oil they squeezed from the seeds filled a big barrel. The younger brother thought he ought to make a present of several bottles of the delicious sesame oil to his older brother, to thank him for the seeds. So he went to the barrel with a pail, but was horrified to find that there was not a drop of oil left in the barrel.

He searched in great fury for the culprit. Eventually he discovered that the culprit was the family dog, just a puppy. The puppy had eaten all the oil, and oil was oozing from its every pore. This infuriated his master, who took him into the forest and hung him from the bough of a tree. Then he yelled with all his might, "Come on, tigers, here's a tasty meal for you!" And he left the forlorn puppy dangling there.

Of course the puppy did not know what he had done wrong. He whimpered and squealed in sorrow and pain. Some tigers heard his cries and began to gather round him. The delicious fragrance of sesame oil whetted their appetite, and finally one tiger jumped up and devoured the puppy in one gulp.

This puppy was so greasy, though, with all the oil oozing out of him, that he passed right through the tiger, rope and all, and out its other end. But he popped right into the mouth of a tiger standing in back of the first tiger. And right out the other end of this tiger, rope

Greased Puppy 187

and all. Soon every tiger there had its chance at the puppy, and every one was strung up on the rope.

The puppy's master came out to the forest the next day to see what had become of his puppy. He could not believe his eyes when he saw how that little puppy had strung all those ferocious tigers on the rope. He ran for the villagers, and they all came and killed and skinned the tigers. And the younger brother lived the rest of his life prosperously.

Thereafter the villagers hung deep-fried ox sinew to tree branches—on the end of a long rope, of course. You might imagine how wealthy that village became.

Confrontations
with Tiger

The Man with the Chessboard Back

One summer some eighty years ago a man by the name of Kang Tŏk-kyo was travelling through the Hongch'ŏn region of Kangwon Province in search of medicinal herbs. He came upon a stream along the dusty country road and, since it was a very hot day, plunged in and enjoyed a refreshing bath.

After a while he decided he had better get back on the road, so he got out and started drying himself in the cool shade of a tree. Just then the stranger who had been bathing upstream from Kang came down the stream toward him. Kang looked once, and then looked twice, because this middle-aged stranger had some strange marks on his back. A third look showed Kang that the marks were scars, which criss-crossed the muscular back and gave it the appearance of a chessboard. Kang was intrigued. He had seen men with tattoos of plum blossoms or dragons on their arms, but never a man with a chessboard on his back.

Barely able to wait until they exchanged the usual greetings of the road, Kang said with wonder, "Forgive my curiosity, but you seem to have a chessboard on your back. How did you get it? Were you born with it?"

Kang's questions triggered some powerful memories

in the man. He was quiet for some time, then answered, "Well, let me tell you then. But I hope you're not squeamish. Even a ghost would be shocked to hear how I got this chessboard of mine."

And this is the adventure the stranger had had many years before.

His name was Pak, and he was from a farming family in Hongch'ŏn. He had married young, but, even before they had children, was soon widowed. Pak could not get another wife and, living alone, did not know the pleasures of family life. Naturally he cared little for staying at home, and his heart was always restless. He was on the wild side to begin with and hated the tediousness of routine farm life. Gradually he began to stay away from home, and soon he took up the life of a peddler. He found this life of travelling the whole country more to his liking than farming. When he was on the road he befriended the more sophisticated fellows in the bigger towns and cities and frequented drinking houses and brothels with his friends any chance he got. So it was a matter of course that he got involved with quite a few professional ladies.

Once Pak made the obligatory visit home for the new year holidays from a trip that had taken up a good part of the winter. Home he came for the holiday season, but it was not a home where he had any wife or cute little children to welcome him. Stuck in the empty house with nothing to do, before a couple of days passed he soon became restless again. And those insistent memories of all his female companions did not help the situation any. So he stayed just a couple of days more and then, not being able to stand it any longer, set out again even before the first full moon. He was headed south for Yŏngju, in Kyŏngsang Province, where his favorite woman lived.

He had his usual back pack, now stuffed with new holiday clothing and quite a few strings of coins. Carrying the bundle on his back he passed through Wonju, Chech'ŏn and Tanyang, and, by the evening of the first full moon, finally made it all the way to the foothills of Chungnyŏng Mountain at the northwest border of Kyŏngsang Province.

There he stopped at a roadhouse he had become familiar with and was treated to a hearty serving of rice brew to celebrate the first full moon. The roadhouse keeper advised him to stay the night on their side of the mountain because it was quite late, but Pak set out again, the lissome image of one Yŏngju woman beckoning to him in the fog of his inebriated mind.

Unaware that it was already midnight, Pak sauntered up the moonlit trail of the steep valley in the high spirits of a drunk. The mountain was quiet, with nothing in sight except the silhouette of the misty peaks covered with their trees. Occasionally a wisp of humid wind licked his face.

"Stop!" First the sudden growling command, and then, with a wild rustling of dry leaves, half a dozen figures leaped out of the trees. They were bandits, no doubt about it. Their faces were all covered with beards, so you couldn't tell one apart from another, not that it would have made any difference. Now Pak was a gutsy man, with the strength to go with it, but he found himself helpless in front of a band of thieves.

"Don't make a move. Hand over that pack."

Pak unshouldered his pack and handed it to them. Not content with the pack, they also demanded the broad hat he was wearing.

"The coat, too. And the pants and shirt."

Pak promptly did as he was told, until he got down to his pants. He could not bring himself to take off these, because he was wearing nothing under them. It would not be so bad in the mountains, but he could imagine how embarrassed he would be walking into the next roadhouse stark naked.

"Come on, the pants too. No? So you think you're man enough to have something there worth seeing, or worth hiding, is it? Well you can keep that, we don't need it. But hand over the pants."

"Please, just let me keep these, I beg you."

"Another word from you, and you've had it." They flaunted their swords and spears in his face.

The choice was obvious when it came down to either his pants or his life, so Pak soon returned to the pristine state in which he was born. A wintry night in the mountains was going to be very difficult to endure with no clothing, but there was not much he could do about it at the moment.

"Come on, he's not worth any more of our time when there's bigger prey elsewhere." So the shadowy figures disappeared over the ridge, leaving Pak immensely relieved to have kept at least his life. It certainly was not easy, though, to travel stark naked, shivering to the bone in the cold wind. To keep from being seen he took a steep, narrow trail rather than the main pass.

The trail was rocky and webbed with thick undergrowth, and he stumbled more than he walked. He had gone about four or five kilometers when he saw a house's light flickering through the trees across the ravine. Strange as it was that someone should be living in such a remote valley, Pak was only too happy to see the light and hoped he could beg at least some rags to cover himself.

As he eagerly approached the light he found that it was actually a cluster of houses there. He went up to the nearest one. Covering himself with his hands, he stood behind the wicket fence and asked in the meekest voice he could manage if the master of the house would come out. After an eternity of calling the door of the house creaked open, but to Pak's great discomfort it was a woman in her undergarments that opened the door.

"Please forgive me, it's so late and everything. But I am a poor traveller, robbed of all my clothes."

The woman paid little attention to what he was saying, being much more interested in the fascinating spectacle of his nudity. Finally, she asked rather tersely, "How did it happen?"

"Well, I was attacked by some bandits on the Chungnyŏng pass, and they took all my clothes. I just barely got away from them, then stumbled down here. If you could kindly give me some clothes..."

He wanted to ask her to let him sleep there, but could not bring himself to ask this much of a woman living by herself. Then the woman murmured, to his great relief, "I can't possibly let you outside all night in weather like this. You'd freeze to death. Come inside."

Pak followed her into the house. No one else was there.

"Please wait in that room there," she told him, disappearing into the main room. She returned in no time with a set of man's clothing, and walked right up to him in his nudity to give him the clothes. Pak saw sparks in those seductive eyes, and, veteran that he was with women, he could not ignore the sign she was giving him. He undressed her in his mind, but she was already gone, back to the main room, before he could do anything more.

And then she came back, with some bedding this time. "You must be freezing. Why don't you get under the cover and warm yourself? But have you had any supper? No, of course not, with all..." she sat down on the floor and chattered away, casually stretching out her legs under the cover she had given him.

He put his legs under the cover too, and she did not seem to mind. They chatted this way for a while, and from what she said and the way she behaved, Pak concluded that this was certainly no ordinary housewife. Looking straight and deep into his eyes, smiling provocatively, she got up and, after peeping out through a hole in the door, firmly bolted the door.

She snuggled down under the covers and beckoned to him with smouldering eyes. Pak needed no further encouragement. She blew out the lamp even before he was all the way under the covers with her. With that light went Pak's last thought of restraining himself against taking another man's wife. After all, as they say, "After every storm comes a rainbow." He congratulated himself for this turn of luck, justifying what he was going to do as providential compensation for the loss he had suffered earlier that night.

The woman whispered, her hot breath tickling his ears, "This sure is a funny world. One man robs another man of his clothes, and then the robbed one turns around and robs the robber of his wife." Pak's heart shrank to a cold lump. Thinking by his silence that he did not understand, she elaborated. "You see, one of the thieves that robbed you must surely be my husband."

Pak was speechless. What bad luck! It was bad enough to be robbed of all his clothes and possessions, but to walk out of that and right into the bandit's den on his own two feet and beg for clothes, and then take the bandit's wife... What a revolting turn of events!

"What am I going to do if your husband comes back?"

"He is too busy robbing people to come home at night."

Even before her reassuring words were out of her mouth, a husky male voice came from outside the house. "Open up!" Pak despaired, sure he was a doomed man. But the woman told him calmly, "Don't worry. You just lie right here, very still. I'll handle him."

The woman dressed quickly and went out to open the gate. "You're early today."

"We called it a day since it's a holiday. Everything all right here?" asked the husky voice, which Pak recognized as one of the thieves'.

"A stark naked man came here begging for clothes. Must be one of your victims."

"So what did you do?"

"I thought it would be better to keep him here than let him go, so I told him he could stay here the night. I put him in the other room."

"Good. I'll take care of him now."

Pak saw his world fast approaching its end.

"Oh, come on. Do we have to smell blood when we go to bed? You can finish him off in the morning."

"That's not a bad idea. But I ought to lock him up nice and tight. Wouldn't want him to go out into that cold night out there." The thief came over to Pak's room and locked the door.

While the thief was dreaming his sweet dreams with his woman snuggled at his side, Pak was dying a slow death of anxiety. There was no window, the door would not budge no matter how hard he pushed, and there was no way for him to break down the wall.

After racking his brain for an inspiration, he finally lifted the coarse mat that covered the earthen floor and urinated, making a puddle. Then he scraped at the wet spot until he got down to the slate stones of the flue that heated the room. He removed a couple of the slabs to make a hole big enough for him to crawl through the flue to its mouth in the fireplace in the kitchen next to his room.

It was a very tight fit, and he had to wriggle a long time before he could make it to the other end. When he finally got there he pushed his head out with a big smile.

Then he stopped smiling. There, crouching and watching Pak with great interest, was a tiger. It seemed to Pak that he had gone quite a bit out of his way to serve himself up to the beast.

The tiger seemed delighted at its good luck. It took

the man in its mouth, yanked him from the fireplace, and flung him on its back. The tiger loped off with its victim into the forest.

It was only when they had got deep into the woods that Pak came to his senses. "Okay now, a tiger has me. And if I don't pull myself together right quick, I'm a goner as sure as can be."

The tiger dumped him onto a rock in front of a cave. In no time its cubs came running out. To make this nightmare even more bizarre, a loud clanging of gongs and cymbals was coming from somewhere in the distance. The big tiger jumped up at the metallic sound and disappeared into the woods, but the cubs were already all over the man's limp body, cutting deep scratches into his back with their claws and feasting on his blood.

Pak suddenly recalled the proverb that one could get out of the clutches of a tiger if only he kept a clear head, so he pulled himself together. Never minding the scathing pain in his sliced up back, he began to kick and batter the cubs until all of them were sprawled lifeless around him. Then he remembered that the mother tiger might return any second now, so he climbed up a tall pine tree that stood by the rock.

He looked down when he got to the top and, sure enough, here came the mother back to her cubs. At the sight of her dead cubs she leaped and raved in distress, her fearsome roars resounding through the woods and valley.

Then she spotted Pak perched up there, hanging on precariously for dear life. Glaring at him with eyes of fiery vengeance, she jumped and jumped to get at him, just missing him with her grasping claws.

She kept on like this through the rest of the night.

The Man with the Chessboard Back 199

About daybreak, though, she stopped, and Pak looked all over for her. He very quietly, very carefully slipped down from the tree, holding his breath, eyes and ears pricked for any sign of the beast. He got down all the way and looked around, finally finding her lying motionless between a large boulder and the stump of a tree.

She was dead. She had impaled herself on the sharp end of a broken branch sticking out from the tree stump. Apparently she had been unable to free herself, wedged in there so firmly between the boulder and the tree.

It turned out that the sound of gongs and cymbals had come from the village down the mountain. A scholar there by the name of Yi had a beautiful and virtuous daughter. He was naturally very careful in selecting a spouse for her. On her wedding night, just a few days ago, the bridegroom had disappeared, carried off by a tiger on his way back from the outhouse.

There was only one tiger that preyed on the village, and that was none other than the one that had carried off Pak. The scholar, afraid that the tiger might come back and get his daughter too, hired the villagers to bang away on their gongs and cymbals every night. On the third night, to the bewilderment of the villagers, the tiger kept roaring as if it were going to tear up the whole valley. So they banged away even louder. Then the roar of the beast stopped abruptly, and was never heard again.

The villagers became suspicious and organized a search party. They were climbing up the mountain to the tiger's den when they heard a man shouting to them that he had killed a tiger. They all rushed up to him and, lo and behold, there stood a strapping young man beside the prostrate body of a huge tiger. The young man was quite calm, even though his back had numerous cuts and he was covered with blood.

When they got over the initial shock, the villagers showered him with questions. "Who in the world are you?" "What happened here?"

"Nothing happened. I just sent a tiger to its death,

that's all." In his cavalier attitude he was telling the people that he himself had taken care of the tiger, that his patience and courage had rid the village of this curse.

The villagers picked up the dead tiger and put Pak on their shoulders and carried the two to Yi's house. When Pak arrived, in all his glory, he passed out from the acute pain that seized him now that he had finally let himself relax. Yi's daughter, believing he was both her avenger and her savior, nursed him with all the care she could give. Having lost her husband on her wedding night, even before the marriage could be consummated, the woman never left the side of the wounded Pak, confident that heaven had sent him to replace the bridegroom she had lost.

And that is how Pak came to marry Yi's daughter and stopped wandering all over the country peddling and womanizing. He settled down and became a farmer, this time quite content.

So now you know the story of how Pak got the chessboard on his back.

How Men Began to Travel with Their Wives

The market opened every five days on Tavern Street beyond the high, long thickly wooded hill to the east of the village. That hill was home to a man-eating tiger which would attack travellers in shadowy nooks even in broad daylight, and quite a few on their way to and from the market had already been gobbled up by it. So even the strongest young men avoided the hill path, preferring the long but safe detour skirting the hill. If the hill path could not be avoided, the villagers formed a party and travelled in a group.

No one ever dared to travel the hill path after sunset. For the unknowing wayfarer who might opt for the shortcut, a sign at the foot of the hill warned: "He who wants to see a man-eating tiger, go this way."

At the end of a certain market day, long after all the shoppers and vendors had gone home, some menfolk were still loitering on the other side of the hill, pleasantly drunk at someone else's expense. It was very late, and no one looked forward to making that long trek back around the hill to their homes on the other side. Some, in fact, wanted to use the hill path.

"Heck, what's the big deal? It's just a tiger. Come on, let's go," urged one whom the brew had made very brave.

"Well, I plan to live a long life. And even though I'm going to have to die someday, I certainly don't want to do it feeding myself to a tiger. I'll need my body all in one piece to get a proper burial."

So the debate went on and on, each man insisting that his route was the best. At that moment they spotted a woman coming out of the woods at the bottom of the hill. She was all alone.

"See, even a woman can take that path all alone, and quite safely at that. Now let's go. There's nothing to be afraid of," said a strapping young man. Everyone agreed and started off. When they met up with the woman, she told them she had heard the menacing and booming roar of a tiger that must have been as big as a mountain.

Those who had been against taking the hill path plopped down right on the spot and refused to move. The woman saw this and clucked at their pitiful display of cowardice, then volunteered to guide them over the hill. "Tsk, tsk, why should you be so scared of a tiger when you are so young and strong? Come with me, boys. I'll take care of the tiger if it comes our way."

The woman turned around and calmly led the way to the path where she said she had seen the tiger. The men were flabbergasted at the woman's bravado, but they were also curious as to why she was not disturbed by the tiger. Some were deathly afraid but managed to contain their fear, their tender male egos already bruised by the woman's condescension. Reluctantly they trudged after the woman and the rest of the party followed at a good distance behind, doubtless trusting that if the tiger attacked them, the woman would be its first target and they would have enough time to run away.

They had not got very far into the woods when a dreadfully big tiger leaped out roaring at them. They had all expected that, and had planned in their minds how they were going to handle it, but thinking about a tiger and looking it right in the eye are two very different things. Not one of the men could move, petrified by fear from head to toes.

Not the woman, though. She walked confidently toward the tiger. Suddenly she flipped her white skirt over her head and crawled on her hands and knees up the slope toward it. The cowering men watched her dumbfounded, but it seemed the most surprised of everyone there was the tiger, who jolted to a stop. It eyed the woman warily for a while, and then slipped away into the darkness of the forest, tail between its legs.

"Ha! What kind of fearsome beast is that? Its huge white mouth is bigger than mine!" The men swore they heard the tiger muttering as it ran away.

The men all nodded their heads, as if they had learned something. From then on, whenever they were so pressed for time that they had to travel the hill path, they never hesitated to do so. All they had to do was take their wives with them and the tiger would never show up.

And that is how men began to travel with their wives.

The Tiger that Learned to Play the Bugle

On one bitterly cold night a young man was traveling in the mountains. Looking for a house to lodge for the night, he spotted a cottage on the nearest ridge and approached it. It was deserted. He had heard people say that tigers frequented deserted houses in the mountains, but he decided to take his chances, thinking that, tiger or no tiger, it would be better to be inside than out on a night like this.

Inside the dusty house the young man hunched in a corner, full of misgivings about his decision, but too cold to go back out. A while later a tiger did indeed show up at the outside gate and, smelling a human, came up to the house. When a tiger enters its cave it backs in, and that is just what it did here.

While it might be less frightening to see a tiger's rear end than its front, the young man knew it was only a matter of time before he would come face to face with the beast. He was beside himself with fear.

He groped in his bundle looking for anything that he could use as a weapon to fight the tiger off, as fight he knew he must, even if it would be futile. He grabbed

206

the bugle that he carried with him always and everywhere, and rammed it up the tiger's rear end. The tiger was, to say the least, surprised. It strained its insides to push the strange object out, only to get the shock of its life when the pressure caused the bugle to blare. The tiger took off running, all the while straining harder to get rid of the bugle, which only made the bugle blare louder, frightening the poor tiger even more and making it run faster and faster.

    The young man was relieved to be alive, but missed his bugle badly. So he followed the tiger, asking people if they had heard a bugle, and from which direction the sound had come. Days later the exhausted young man calculated the tiger must have run about a thousand *ri* that night.

Tiger Indigestion

One fine spring day an honest and diligent hunter went quite deep into the mountains for game. Coming upon a flat rock warmed by the sun, he lay down on it to take a nap. And he fell into a deep, sweet sleep.

A tiger passed by the rock and, rejoicing at its good fortune, grabbed the man and dragged him to its den, where a whole family of tigers lived.

The oldest and largest of the tigers glared at each of the tigers and asked, "Boys, what should we do with this food? If anyone has a good idea how to divide it evenly, speak up."

Various ideas and opinions were tossed around until one said, "It's too little to split up among so many of us. It'll be no more than an appetizer, and our stomachs wouldn't know if the tiny morsel even went in or not. So Boss, we think you should eat it yourself."

All the tigers agreed and the Boss swallowed the hunter in one gulp.

The hunter woke up from his nap to find that he was in a long, spacious cavern of some sort. "I'm sure this is the inside of a tiger. And I'm sure that I'm still alive. What I'm not sure of is how I'm going to get out of here."

Tiger Indigestion

After some thinking, he took his knife from his pocket and began cutting the tiger's belly. The tiger jumped with pain, screaming how it must have eaten poison. The pain became worse and worse and finally drove the tiger out of its mind. It kicked, bit and tore apart whatever got in its way. After a while, most of the tigers lay dead and the Boss lay unconscious.

The hunter finally cut all the way through the tiger's belly and climbed out. He gathered up all the dead tigers and amassed a fortune by selling their skins.

Another hunter, this one greedy and lazy, heard the news and went to that very same rock. He slept on it like the honest hunter did, so that he too could become rich. A cousin of the tiger that ate our honest hunter spotted this dishonest hunter, and brought him back to its den. But the tigers had learned a hard lesson from their previous experience with humans. Instead of gulping down the hunter in one mouthful, they divided him into little pieces so every one of the pack could have a bite.

And so the lazy hunter, who wanted to make a fortune without working for it, thus disappeared without a trace.

A Woman's Way

Once in about the sixteenth century, at the middle of the Chosŏn dynasty, on a remote mountain in Kangwon Province, a lone traveler was walking along a deserted trail at sunset. He was carrying a big, heavy load on his back. His face was covered with a scraggly growth of whiskers. He did not appear much over thirty, but he was very tired, trudging under his heavy load like a man twice his age. The sun was setting and he still had one more ridge to go before he would come to any human dwelling.

Reaching the foot of the slope, he sat heavily down on a boulder and muttered, "Darn! Another day gone by with almost nothing to show for it. I should have decreased this load of salt today, but all I've accomplished is to increase the walking. And I have such a long way to go, and it's already getting dark. What rotten luck!"

Yes, he was a salt peddler, backpacking salt from village to village. Dragging his complaining feet, he forced himself back on the road. The sun was gone completely by the time he made it half way up the ridge and, being in the mountains, it was very soon so dark that he could not see where he was going.

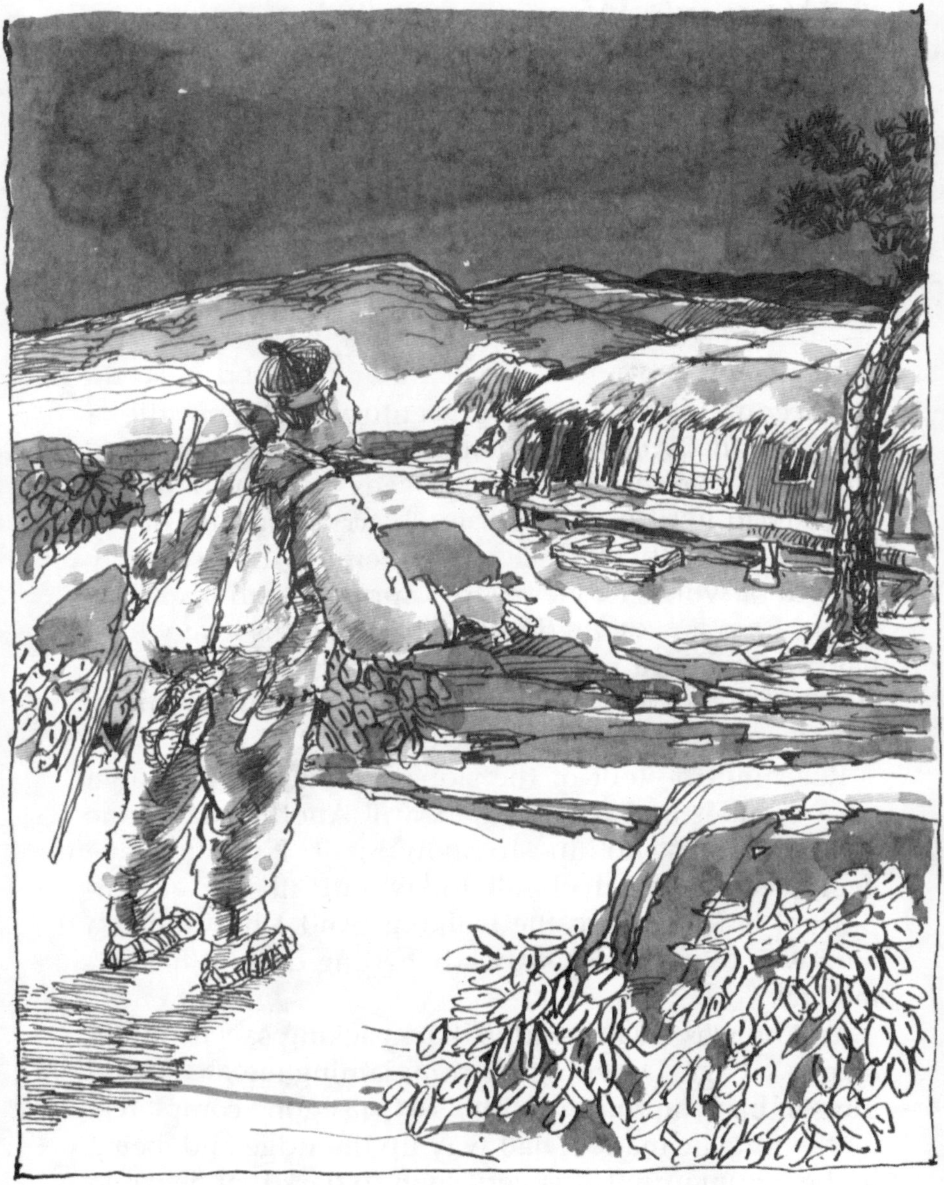

It was the end of the month and in the moonless sky the stars were shimmering. Shadowy trees loomed like devils about to grab him. Shivers ran up and down his spine. As he plodded along he strained his eyes to see into the darkness ahead.

At long last he spotted a faint glimmer of light near the top of the ridge. He hastened toward the light, keeping his eyes on it lest he lose sight of it.

When he got closer he found that the light was coming from a shabby, dilapidated shack, which seemed to be a hunter's dwelling. Rejoicing at his good luck, the peddler pounded on the door and shouted happily, "Hello, hello! Anybody home?"

A response came quite promptly from inside and a woman in her thirties appeared at the door. "Who are you, and at such a late hour?"

"I'm very sorry for bothering you at this time of the night. I am a peddler. Would you please let me stay the night here?"

"Well, I really don't know what to say. My husband's not back yet from the market. Did you happen to see anyone on the way?"

"No, I saw neither man nor beast. It would have been nice if I had come across someone, so I wouldn't have had to walk alone in the dark like that."

"Ah, well. Please come in, anyway, if you can put up with this meager dwelling."

The peddler was embarrassed to force himself on the woman in the absence of the man of the house, but it was quite obvious that he could not stay outside till the man returned. So, mumbling an apology, he followed her inside.

The woman left him and soon returned with some boiled potatoes. "We've got nothing besides potatoes out here, so far away from everything. But please, you must be starved. Help yourself."

To his empty stomach the potatoes tasted far better than the meat and rice he was used to, and in no time he had eaten all of them. When he finished eating it seemed there was nothing for him or his hostess to do except wait for the master of the house to return. The woman huddled in a deep corner of the room, worrying why her husband was not coming back. The peddler sat uncomfortably near the door. Then he fell asleep, snoring loudly.

The woman became more and more worried as time went by. When she could not stand it any longer she went over to the man and shook him. "Wake up, sir. Please wake up."

It took a lot of hollering and shaking for her to get the tired peddler to open his eyes, but he became wide awake as soon as he realized he had been sleeping in someone else's home.

"I'm sorry to disturb you," the woman said, "but my husband isn't back yet. I'm afraid something dreadful has happened to him. I've heard tigers are especially rampant these days and I'm sorry to bother you, but wouldn't you please come with me and help find him?"

It was more an order than a request, regardless of the polite way she said it. But the peddler, frightened at even the mention of tigers, grumbled, "What can we do in the dead of night? Can't see a thing. It won't do any good. Let's wait till daybreak to look for him."

"By then all that'll be left of him is his bones. We must start right now."

The woman busily got ready. Finding no excuse to refuse further, the peddler followed her, reluctantly. She handed him an axe, lit a torch for herself, and said,

"Follow me."

After wandering around some time through the woods, up and down the mountain trails, they came across a piece of cloth caught on the branch of a tree. It was soaked with blood, but the woman knew it was part of her husband's clothes. She turned pale and gritted her teeth. It was obvious he had been attacked by a tiger. They followed the bloody trail for a while, when suddenly the peddler gasped at the two fierce eyes of a tiger glaring at him. Blood was still fresh on its mouth, and under his paws was sprawled the mauled body of a man.

The woman stepped up to the tiger, her eyes ablaze. "You wretched brute, you're not going to fatten yourself on my husband's flesh. Never!" And with a shrill cry, she whacked the tiger between the eyes with her ax.

The tiger dropped dead just like that. The woman collected what remained of her husband. Tears streaming down her face, she said to the peddler, "We have to take him home. Will you follow me with the torch? Or do you want to go first with the body?"

The peddler fidgeted a while, then shouldered the corpse and walked ahead of her. When they arrived at the house, the woman laid the body in the room, then went out to the yard and began to whet the ax until the blade gleamed cold and sharp. The peddler was gripped with fear.

"What are you going to do with that ax? The tiger's dead."

"For the same reason I walked behind you with the torch. That tiger I killed was a male. Its mate will surely try to get revenge. It should, too, the same as I killed its mate to avenge my mate. I can understand, because a wife's heart works the same way, human or beast. That

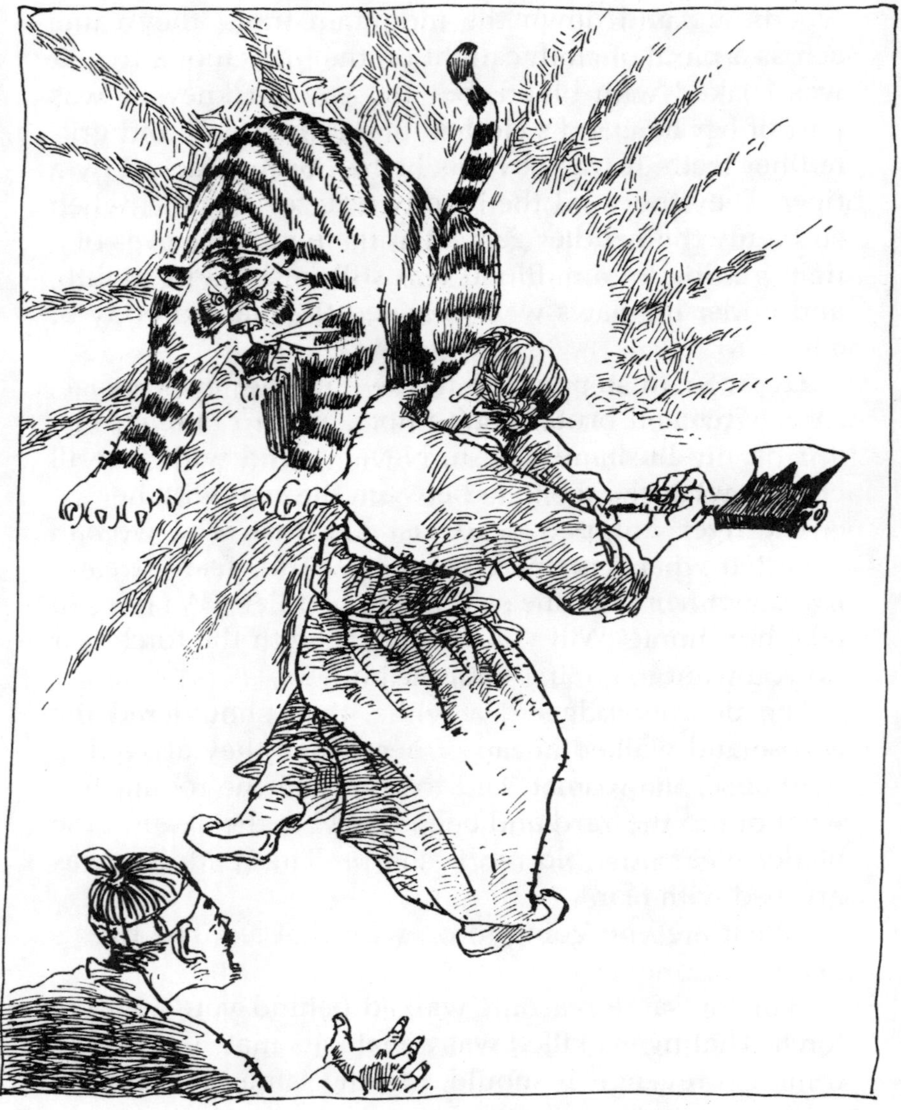

she tiger and I are mortal foes now, and it's not over till one of us is dead."

Towards daybreak, with a furious roar that shook the mountains and shattered the sky, a tigress appeared at the house. Its roar scared the peddler out of his wits and chilled even the marrow in his bones.

While the man was shrinking back like one at the brink of hell, the woman was calmness itself. She'd been waiting all night for this moment. She stepped out into the yard, the gleaming ax gripped in her hand.

The eyes of the woman and the tiger clashed, icy enough to freeze the world and hot enough to thaw it back. Neither one showed a second thought. The tiger beat the earth and howled. The blade of the woman's ax glinted gold in the rising sun. Then, with a roar, the tiger leaped at the woman. She sidestepped it. The desperate urgency of each to avenge the death of her mate seemed to give each one supernatural energy. Each glared at the other with piercing eyes, trying to fathom the other's mind.

Then, as the sun rose above the east ridge, the woman suddenly let out a fierce yell and whacked the tiger with her ax. The tiger, almost as big as a small mountain, collapsed with a thud. The woman threw away her ax and gazed down at her foe for a long time, as if she had turned to stone. Then she lifted her eyes to heaven and wept her heart out.

The salt peddler, not wishing to witness any more of these gruesome scenes, hurried to leave. The woman stopped him. "Thank you very much for helping me avenge my husband," she said, and gave him four rolls of fine cloth and five strings of coins. "It's not much, but please take these as a token of my gratitude. They are of no use to me now."

The peddler accepted them gratefully, and departed. When he reached the ridge he turned back for one last look at the place. The woman was setting fire to her house. Then she walked into the room where she had laid her husband. The next minute, the house was engulfed in blazing flames.

The peddler was so shocked he nearly collapsed, and the coins fell from his hand and rolled away. The sun was already high up when he started on his way again. Now he trudged along even more wearily than the day before. And he kept glancing back at the thin streak of smoke curling up from where the house had been.

And he muttered, "Like a dream. What a woman. What a tiger."

Greedy and Stupid Tiger

Tiger Ingrate

Long, long ago, deep in the mountains of Hwanghae Province, there lived a young man who was very devoted to his mother. His father, once a magistrate, had been a man of learning and integrity and taught his son to be always virtuous and sincere. He had passed away quite unexpectedly, while his son was very young, and mother and son had to live on the little he had left them. When this was gone, they had to move deep into the mountains to find some free land.

On their small plot of land the mother learned to grow crops to support the two. Their land yielded very little, and the mother often had to go without food so that there would be enough to nourish her son so he could concentrate on his studies. The boy studied hard, and even decided not to marry till he succeeded in first passing the national civil service examination and then regaining what wealth that the family used to have.

Ten years of such hardship passed, and the son was now over twenty. It was time for him to see the world and take the examination. He bade farewell to his mother and headed for Seoul. It was a long way, but he plodded on with the dream of passing the exam with the highest honors. He walked all day and at night lodged in houses along the way.

On the tenth night of his journey he found himself deep in the forest of a mountain, with no sign of anyone living nearby. The tranquil beauty of pristine nature gave him such a feeling of power that he composed an impromptu poem. While he was thus engaged, he suddenly heard the howl of a big animal not too far away. He shuddered at the sound, and the magical images of his poem vanished. As frightened as he was, though, his curiosity got the better of his fear and he went to find out what could have made such a mighty sound.

He soon found that it was a tiger. But what could have made the king of the mountains cry so? He drew closer and discovered the tiger trying desperately to get out of a deep hole. The young man thought it a pity and went down to the village where he had slept the night before, and obtained a thick coil of rope to hoist the tiger out of the trap.

He finally got the tiger out. But just as soon as the tiger came up over the rim of the hole he jumped at the scholar and tried to devour him. The scholar jumped out of the way, and shouted at the tiger, "What a waste of time trying to help such an ungrateful beast! To try to make me your meal after I saved you like that...!"

So the scholar challenged the tiger to establish a tribunal to decide who was in the right. "We'll just ask a passerby if it is just to eat someone who has saved your life."

The tiger was rather impatient to get on with its meal, but thought it would humor the scholar for a while and work up a really good appetite. So the two told a nearby pine tree their story and waited in expectation for a just pronouncement.

The pine tree finally said, "After all, hunger must be

satisfied."

Hearing this the victorious tiger pounced at the scholar for the first bite.

But the scholar dodged the tiger again and insisted on a second opinion. So they asked a blackbird perched there on the pine tree. The blackbird, itself eager for a piece of human flesh, replied "Well, if one is hungry, one must eat. If I were you, tiger, I would have eaten him right away."

Now the tiger lunged at the young scholar again, and again the scholar was too quick for him. The scholar knew, though, that he could not go on like this for long, and if he did not use his wits he would soon be the tiger's meal.

"All right, so be it. But as my last wish, let me just have one more opinion."

"No matter how many times you ask, the answer will always be the same," the tiger growled, now at the end of his patience.

Just then a fox happened on by, and the scholar called out to it. "Hey there, fox, we would like to get your opinion. Now please think it over carefully before you answer."

"All right. Shoot."

The scholar earnestly told the fox what was going on there. The fox, after hearing the whole account, squinted and said it could not understand. The scholar thought the fox was just reluctant to give an answer, so he told the fox the whole story again. He told it as simply as he could, but again the fox just squinted and shook his head.

"I really don't understand what you mean," the fox said. "I don't understand well enough to judge. Why not show me just how it happened instead of telling me, from the very beginning? Maybe then I can help you."

The impatient tiger, eager for a quick reply, jumped back in the hole and started explaining how it had all started.

Then the fox said, "Well, this settles everything. Now that the two of you are right back where you started you have no cause for dispute."

The scholar thanked the fox, and continued on his journey to Seoul. And the tiger growled and roared on and on, but no one would listen.

Tiger and Rabbit

One day a famished tiger came across a rabbit. With great delight, he said, "Hello there, Rabbit! What a pleasure! But I regret to say that you will have to be my lunch today."

"Why do you regret it? It will be my pleasure, Mr. Tiger! Oh, but first I just want to ask if you have ever experienced the scrumptious taste of rock cakes."

"Rock cakes?"

"I have just had one, and it was such a pleasure nothing could ever equal it. So life is going to be one big culinary bore from now on, and I don't mind leaving it. But you..."

"Rock cakes? You mean rock like in stone?"

"Rock, like in stone. They look just like ordinary rocks but, oh boy, do they taste good! Of course you have to toast them on an open fire if you want to get that special flavor."

"Sounds like quite a bother to me."

"Yes, it is a bit of a bother. But before you eat me, why don't you just let me give you a taste. You just help me get a fire started and I'll take care of the rest."

So Tiger got to work lighting the fire. Meanwhile Rabbit collected eleven big stones and threw them into

Tiger and Rabbit 225

the fire.

When the stones were red hot Rabbit exclaimed, "Oh, but we forgot the soy sauce! Let me quickly run down to the village to get some. I'll be back in a jiffy. But don't you dare eat even a single one of them without me. I want just one more before..."

"What do you take me for anyway? Don't you worry, Rabbit."

"Just want to make sure. Now, there are exactly ten, right? So let's see ten there when I get back." And she scampered off.

After Rabbit left the rapacious Tiger felt even hungrier. He looked at the glowing stones again and again, and finally discovered there were eleven.

"Hah! That dumb Rabbit miscounted! I might as well eat the extra one before she gets back." So he gulped down the blazing hot stone.

One can guess what followed. After all, what would anyone do with a red hot rock in your stomach?

Tiger took a dive into the nearest pond and guzzled up all the water.

A few months later, in a wide dry reedy fen, Tiger ferreted out Rabbit. Still hungry, and twice as angry, Tiger jumped on Rabbit. "Gotcha!"

But the ever glib Rabbit cried out, "Mr. Tiger! Wherever did you go that day? I've been looking all over for you!"

"Yeah, well here I am, buster. And here you are. So let's get back to where we started."

"But of course! I have lived through thick and thin and am weary of this life. To offer my measly flesh to you, such an honor! Such a... Oh, but there is one thing. It would be such a shame if my wits, which could be of some service to you, were to be eaten along with my flesh."

"You think I'm pretty dumb, huh?"

"Now if you will just calm down for a minute... Eat scrawny little old me, and your appetite will be back raging again in just a few minutes. I'm going to show you a way to satisfy your appetite this time, and forever after. Then you can eat me."

"Okay, but make it fast. This appetite's been waiting long enough as it is."

"As you can see, there are many sparrows flying around. I will shoo them straight into your mouth. All you have to do is open your jaws very, very wide, close your eyes, and wait."

Tiger could already taste the tender crunchy sparrows in his mouth, and after that Rabbit. So he opened his jaws as wide as he could, and waited.

Rabbit scurried off. A few minutes later, Tiger could hear a crackling sound. Rabbit had set fire to the fen, but the rapacious Tiger mistook the sound of the crackling flames for the sound of birds and he just kept on waiting, jaws wide open.

When it started to get suspiciously hot, Tiger opened his eyes and looked around. Too late. The flames jumped at his fur and held on, so he ran, and the faster he ran the stronger the flames burned. He saw a pond up ahead and dived in, and came back up looking like a piece of charcoal.

As fate would have it, Tiger and Rabbit met again one day on a dam across a river. Rabbit saw Tiger first, though, and pretended not to notice. Right on the spot she contrived another trick. She dipped her cottonball tail in the river, and just sat there.

Tiger was furious that Rabbit was sitting there so calm at the approach of the King of Beasts, and gave a ferocious growl to make her tremble with trepidation and remorse.

"Dear me! Mr. Tiger, look at what you've just done! If only you had kept silent for another five minutes, I would have on this humble tail as many fish as sorghum grains in a sorghum sack!"

"Okay Rabbit, what cute trick do you have up your sleeve this time?" But Tiger's mouth watered at the thought of those fresh, tender fish. Poor creature, if he only knew how many mortals have been driven to ruin on account of their appetite.

"Trick? Me? I'm just catching fish, like I told you."

"Hmm. Now how do you do that?"

"Oh, just follow my instructions. All you need is a little patience to give the fish ample time to know you're there. Because when they come, they come in hordes. Let me just show you how. Now, you drop that handsome long tail of yours in the water and be as still as you possibly can, until I say when. If you move before I tell you to it'll all come to nothing. Remember that!"

As night drew on the river began to freeze. Tiger felt a tug at his tail and thought it was the weight of the fish that he was feeling. He drooled with expectation. Although he had been very patient and still for such a long time, Rabbit gave no sign to pull it in. When Tiger looked at Rabbit imploringly, all Rabbit would do was put her finger to her lips and wink.

At the crack of dawn Tiger at last decided that he had had enough of waiting and tried to pull his tail out of the water. It pulled back at him. Tentatively peering over his shoulder, he found the river frozen solid and his tail stuck fast in it.

The miserable Tiger could not break the ice, and he certainly did not want to cut off his proud tail. He could not cut it off even if he wanted to. So he called desperately for Rabbit, and Rabbit responded. She laughed and scampered off, and didn't stop laughing until she could be heard no more. And who knows if she stopped even then?

The forlorn Tiger was found in the morning by some young men of the village who had to cross the river to their fields. Too bad Tiger did not have Rabbit's wits.

Tiger Whiskers

Way back in the old days man had at least some intellect, but no courage. Heaven therefore created the tiger, so that man might learn courage from it.

The long whiskers of the tiger were so thin that they were almost invisible, but once they came in contact with its prey they were powerful enough to impale and kill it. So people began to discuss how they could defeat the tiger.

After a long debate the men decided to send some clever women to a nearby band of tigers to learn the secret source of their courage. So the lovely young women went up to the tigers, who were basking in the warm sunshine of spring, especially comfortable after a long winter. The women came up close to the tigers and, with all the sweetness they could summon, said, "Honorable tigers! We fervently respect your awesome roar that sends all creatures shivering and scurrying, and so we would like to offer you our sincerest expression of homage. You would be doing us a big honor to accept it." Then all the women clasped their hands demurely and bowed deeply.

The tigers were bewildered, but at the same time very pleased, and their mouths opened wide in a grin. "So sweet and so beautiful! Your young hearts and fresh faces are a delight to behold!" The tigers pulled back their whiskers so the ladies would not prick themselves on them.

"So why do you come to us with such compliments? One begins to wonder if there is no ulterior motive..."

"Oh, no! Our men, on whom we depend for protection, lack courage and they are sometimes afraid to do what must be done. We would like to help them, but we lack the knowledge. So we have come to ask you to kindly teach us how we can make our men strong. In return we will fill your hours of boredom with song and dance."

The women broke up into two groups. Some sang while the others danced to the song. The tigers were soon gaily dancing with them and laughing heartily. "Ah ha! This is great! So many pretty girls dancing and singing like this for us. Here, have some courage if you want!" And the tigers cut off their whiskers and stuck them on the chins of the women.

The whiskered women returned to the village, delighted that their plan had worked so well. Once back, some of the women started to feel that giving these whiskers of courage to the men after all their trouble would be unfair. It was they who had risked their lives to obtain the secret, and why should they turn this new power over to their men? So a debate started amongst the women as to whether they should or should not hand these whiskers over to their men.

The men started to woo the women to get the whiskers. And thus began the tradition of the male wooing the proud female.

The women still did not turn over their new prize to the men. But later, when they cuddled their babies close to their bosoms, their whiskers poked and scratched the babies. So they realized and then regretted their selfishness and pride, and gave the whiskers to the men.

These new whiskers gave the men courage and strength, and even dignity. And ever since then whiskers have been a symbol of authority.

Tiger Dung

The Bald Drummer

Mun-gwang Township in Koesan County, North Ch'ungch'ŏng Province, was well known for its good hunting. One night some people were chatting in the house of one of their neighbors. Among them was an old man whose head was strangely devoid of any hair, and he had an ugly scar on his forehead as if he had been scalded.

"Grandpa, please tell us the story of how you got your bald head."

"But how many times have I told you already?"

"And it gets better every time you tell it."

Grinning with pride, the old man started his tale.

He had lived all of his seventy years in Yŏsaeng Village and had never even been to another place. When he was in his mid-twenties there was a renowned female shaman in the village. She knew what a wild, fearless, fun-loving young man he was, and always asked him to beat the gongs and drums whenever she did an exorcism. He also joined in her ritual dance, which never failed to make it twice as powerful.

One day the shaman had to perform an exorcism in Panushil, a small village just over the great Kult'i Pass. As usual, our young man was supposed to help her out.

But his wife was very sick, so he was hesitant about going. The shaman, though, begged him to help her, for she had no one else to beat the drums. Reluctantly the young man followed her with the heavy load of equipment for the ritual, determined to get back home that night.

The exorcism ended about one in the morning. The young man announced that he would have to be going back right away, but the villagers told him to stay the night lest he meet with a tiger on the way. He could not stay away from his wife any longer, though, so he started for home, again laden with the gongs and drums, but this time some rice cakes too, from the villagers. He was also quite drunk from all he had had to drink during the course of the ritual.

When he was almost at the summit of Kult'i Pass he felt he could not move another step. "Gee, I can't take this anymore. I'd better get some rest before I try to go any further." So he climbed to the very summit of the pass, made a bed of bush clover, and fell into a deep sleep, with the gongs and drums beside him.

He had been sleeping for some time when he felt something wet on his face. He opened his eyes, and saw the tail of a tiger crossing back and forth over his face. And there was a huge tiger on the other end of it.

Tigers do this to a person when they want to eat him. It lulls the person into a kind of stupor, so they do not scream and kick so much and spoil what could be a delightful meal.

The man knew what the tiger was up to, and he was so terrified he could not move a muscle. But he was able to think, and think he did.

While the tiger was off getting some more water on its tail the young man quickly got hold of his gong.

Then he just waited quietly for the tiger to return. The tiger came back and started whisking its wet tail over the man's face again, and kept this up until the tail dried out. So it turned to go and wet its tail again, and right then the young man smashed on his gong with all his might.

The shocked tiger bolted off, spurting back a mess of red dung. Unfortunately, some of it got on the man's head and face. Now tiger dung is pretty hot stuff, especially when the tiger is scared. So it burned the man's face and later even caused his hair to fall out.

And that is why the old grandfather never forgets to thank his lucky stars for every new day.

A Face in Exchange for a Son

Back in the last century there lived a young farmer in a village at the foot of Mount T'aegye. This mountain, in a township on the way from Hoengsŏng to Sokch'o, was the most heavily forested mountain in all of Kangwon Province.

Fate smiled on this young farmer. He married a pretty woman, and they had a handsome son. But then fate frowned. His wife died when the boy was three years old. In spite of his grief, the young farmer lived his days with great hopes for his son.

One night, when the boy was five, the farmer was just falling asleep after a long, tiring day. His little son whimpered.

"What's the matter?"

"I have to go to the toilet."

Sleepy and tired, the farmer told the boy to go outside and do his duty. The child was scared to go out alone in the dark, but he knew he really had no choice.

· Soon after the boy went out his father heard the boy shriek. He jumped up and rushed outside.

The boy was nowhere to be seen. The farmer guessed that a tiger had gotten his son, because he had heard there was a huge tiger cave in the mountain twenty *ri* from the village.

Without a second thought he dashed off toward the tiger's cave to find his son. Making his way over the mountain pass in the dark, he finally reached the cave. He carefully stepped inside.

Fortunately the tiger was not in the cave. But his child was! The boy had not been killed, not even injured. He was lying unconscious on the ground. Of course, the farmer just wanted to pick up his child and get on back home, but he could not because the tiger could attack them at any point on the way. One false move and both of them would be goners. So he decided to confront the tiger, face to face.

After a long time the tiger finally appeared. Now the tiger is known to be the bravest animal in the mountains, but it is actually quite a coward. So, when it enters some enclosed place it sticks its tail in first and swishes it around to check if everything is safe.

As the farmer attentively watched, the tail touched his hand. The farmer grabbed the tail with both hands. The surprised tiger did its best to pull its tail back, but the farmer held on to it for all he was worth. The tiger could not turn on the man because the cave entrance was too cramped.

As the farmer pulled in with all his strength the tiger pulled out with all its strength. After a long tug-of-war both were exhausted. The tiger, thinking, "If I lose my tail I die tomorrow," put its last ounce of strength into a final ferocious struggle.

The farmer did not let loose, and was knocked against the stone sides of the cave, which bashed and bloodied his whole face.

In desperation, he let go with one hand and rammed that hand up the tiger's rear end, all the way up to its intestines. He clamped down hard, and the startled tiger leapt forward with such force that all its intestines were pulled out and left behind in the man's hand. And the farmer keeled over, exhausted and unconscious.

When he came to, dawn was breaking. He picked up his son and left the cave. Outside he found the corpse of the tiger lying there. He wanted to bring the tiger back for its skin, but he could not carry the tiger by himself. So he went back to the village and got someone to help. Even after he shared the money he got for the tiger skin there was still enough left over for him and his son to lead a more comfortable life.

The farmer knew that if he remained in the village the tiger's mate would surely hunt him down for revenge. So he sold the tiger skin and moved to Seoul. There he worked as a water carrier and devoted all his strength to getting an education for his son.

One day his son confessed something to him. "Father, I have a shameful question, and it will hurt you. But

I've got to ask it."

His father knew what was coming. "Go on, then."

"Why is your face so ugly? My friends run away when they see you coming, and they're always teasing me. I'm going to die of shame. Please tell me why."

The father calmly explained to his son what had happened all those years ago. Realizing that his father had risked his life to save him and endured all the jeers over all these years on his account, the son studied very hard to live up to his father's expectations. And he became a great man, greater than one can be without having known such a father.